ANOTHER FEATHER IN ME CAP

A. Rifleman

COUNTRY BOOKS

Published by Country Books,
Courtyard Cottage, Little Longstone, Bakewell, Derbushire DE45 1NN
on behalf of:
S Belcher, 19 Poplar Lane, Cannock, Staffordshire WS11 1NQ

ISBN 1 898941 18 1

© 1998 S Belcher text and photographs

British Library Cataloguing in Publication Data:
a catalogue record for this book is available from the British Library.

DEDICATION

Thanks to my friends, the sons of Johann Jedinger, for providing the
pictures of the P.O.Ws in Austria from their fathers album to
illustrate this book, that I dedicate to all the good comrades and
friends that made this part of my life worthwhile.

Design, typesetting and production by:
Dick Richardson, Country Books, Little Longstone DE45 1NN

Printed and bound in England by:
MFP Design & Print, Manchester M32 0JT

Origination by:
GA Graphics, Stamford, Lincolnshire PE9 2RB

CONTENTS

Chapter 1
IN THE BEGINNING   5

Chapter 2
CALLED UP INTO THE ARMY   7

Chapter 3
IRELAND   11

Chapter 4
I JOIN THE LONDON IRISH RIFLES   17

Chapter 5
MALVERN   29

Chapter 6
SUMMER IN SUSSEX   34

Chapter 7
NORFOLK   40

Chapter 8
NORTH OF THE BORDER   44

Chapter 9
PREPARING FOR ACTION   50

Chapter 10
NORTH AFRICA   56

Chapter 11
CAPTIVITY — BEHIND THE WIRE   70

Chapter 12
MAKING THE BEST OF IT   78

Chapter 13
TO HELL AND BACK   83

Chapter 14
LIFE IN AUSTRIA   89

Chapter 15
FREE AT LAST   122

Chapter 16
DEMOB   126

Chapter 1

IN THE BEGINNING

Life was beginning to get pretty good in the late 1930s. There was plenty of work, plenty of play, and very few things to worry about, so that the problems of Europe that we saw on film newsreels, and heard on the radio, were far removed from life that was becoming very pleasant. We cared very little for what this upstart of a painter and decorator Adolf Hitler was doing in Germany. Had we not recently beaten them in a war? Were they not bankrupt? and too poor to engage in war? The tanks and the guns that we saw on the films were of course wooden models, so that we were so sure that nothing was going to ruin the good times that we were now old enough and capable of enjoying, such as, plenty of sport, dancing, a few beers, and the girls. Life had at last become worth living, so that it did not seem so terrible when it was announced that all males who had reached their twentieth birthday but not their 21st were to register for National Service. They were required to do six months in the regular forces or four years in the territorial army, and this registration was to take place on Saturday the third of June 1939 in the Sunday school building of the Methodist Chapel at Cannock, that had in earlier years served as the labour exchange where the miners had to sign on for their dole money.

So it was on the appointed day, which was a beautiful sunny Saturday, as a true loyal countrymen I attended to register, and having done so, and always being a nosey person, I spotted some forms that stated that anyone wishing for an exemption or a deferment should fill one in. So I did, not attaching too much importance to it at the time, and awaited developments. In no time at all this letter arrived instructing me to present myself once again to the Methodist Chapel, where a tribunal was to be held to decide on a few applications including mine.

On the Saturday morning of the hearing I arrived to find that I was one of the six or seven who were to be interviewed. A couple of them were accompanied by their mothers who were widows, and they were the main source of income for the family; one other had his wife and baby present; and the others had what I considered to be reasonable reasons for exemptions. While they were all being interviewed, and each application being rejected, I was racking my mind how to explain a good reason for my application. Luckily I was the last one to be interviewed which gave me some extra time, but my hopes of success were sinking as each one of the others was turned down. Lastly I was called in and saw three venerable gentleman sitting behind a long table. I felt like the 'little blue boy' in the picture standing before them, and began by saying, "I have a proposition to make to you, my work is pretty good at this time of the year as I am able to work longer hours in the good weather, the work is far more enjoyable and I am also able to earn more money. In the winter it is awful for working outside building, with lost time, a generally miserable occupation and for less money. "Would you please call me up for service after about the middle of October until the spring of next year? This would seem to be common sense and less of a problem." After a short conference and debate amongst themselves they agreed. "Why not? Request granted!" I could not believe my luck, but that was the day that I reckon the extraordinary bits of luck that happened throughout my war service began and was to continue as I will seek to demonstrate in this story.

Chapter 2
CALLED UP INTO THE ARMY

I had hoped that having settled for a deferment, I could now settle down to all the enjoyment that had been available before, but the dark clouds of war that were gathering more quickly than we had thought they would, rather upset this. In no time at all the summer had gone, and that awful Sunday of the third of September arrived. It started as the usual Sunday morning, having a lie in, after a good Saturday night out. "Mom" as usual was busy in the kitchen, the pile of rock cakes was growing, the pastry was made and the pies were ready for the oven . A good fire was going, and a joint of the best-end of brisket of beef was already beginning to sizzle in the oven. The veg. were all prepared and the radio was switched on to hear the broadcast by Mr Chamberlain that we had been warned about and, were not particularly looking forward to what we were about to hear.

As those fatal words came over the air "We are in a state of war with Germany," I noticed Mom looked around the family as a tear trickled down her cheek. She quickly brushed this away and was busy once again with her cooking. The one thing that I am sure of is that she did not consider them to be chores as the thing she really enjoyed was looking after her family, especially on a Sunday, as she worked hard all the week in the shop that she had recently acquired. The comfort of knowing that I should not be called up for service until

October, and then thinking that I would be having a six months holiday at the Government's expense, quickly vanished. Very shortly after the outbreak of war I was informed that all deferments had been cancelled, and instructions would follow telling me what action I must take.

The work on the two schools where I was in engaged continued at apace, and instructions were given that air raid shelters would be built on the playing fields. This was to be done on a time and material costs system, and this required that records were to be kept, and that supervision was given to it, so that I was promoted to Assistant Foreman to carry out these duties at the princely sum of one penny per hour extra. Days turned into weeks, and weeks turned into winter. The poor sods who had been called up originally to the forces, were now in France, living under canvas, up to their knees in mud, and having a most uncomfortable time. The only consolation being that there seemed to be a stalemate in the action in France. I was beginning to feel uncomfortable about the fact that I still had not joined the forces, but made the most of my good fortune. This lasted throughout the winter into the spring when, at last the buff envelope arrived instructing me to go to Stafford for a medical examination, and an assessment to determine which branch of the forces I would be most suitable for. This was quite a new experience for me, naked men running around from one medical officer to another, having various parts of ones body tested, but the most important part seemed to be "was everything there? And was I breathing?" Having been satisfied of this, and like most of the other fellows not being able to provide a specimen on request, I was told to get dressed and informed that I was A1. I was then passed through for an interview with a couple of officers who inquired about the work that I had always done and what qualifications I had achieved in my working life. They decided that I was most suitable for the Royal Engineers and this seemed to be quite a sensible suggestion so that I would have some idea of the duties that I would be required to carry out. I was then informed that I could now leave and that further instructions would follow in the post, so dashing to the nearest gents I was very surprised, and amused, to find that all the lads who could not provide a specimen were now breaking their necks and heaving a great sigh of relief.

It was early April when the dreaded letter arrived instructing me to present myself to Fullwood Barracks in Preston to join the army. Having said goodbye to all my friends I joined a train at the local station and found a carriage in which there were two young fellows who were obviously going to join up, so we naturally got into conversation. They came from the Birmingham area and we soon became friends. On arriving in Preston there was a steady stream of young gentleman all heading in the same direction carrying their small suitcases, and looking rather apprehensive as to what their future would bring. We were soon left in no doubt about that when we got into the barracks and the N.C.Os. started to bark their orders.They quickly rounded us up into three groups that were to go to three different regiments in Ireland.

At this I started to protest "I am supposed to be joining the Engineers!" then I quickly learned that you do not argue with the orders given to you, even by a lowly Lance Corporal. When they shout, "Fall in over there with that lot", that is what you do and argument seems to be of no avail. So it was I found myself in the group destined for the Royal Ulster Rifles in Armagh.

A line of double-decker buses was standing waiting for us to board to transport us to Stranraer where we were to cross on the ferry to Northern Ireland. Then came the first introduction to army food. We were each handed a package of sandwiches, and a hard boiled egg to last us through the journey. Was that a shock? Slabs of bread like doorsteps, and a green egg, but it is surprising what you will eat when you are hungry, and there was very little left by the end of the journey.

We had to cross during the hours of darkness so this was a fine initiation into the ways of the forces, as it was not considered that one night of missed sleep was of any particular importance.

Feeling pretty fed up, and knackered, we arrived at the barracks at mid-morning the following day. This was some initiation into the British army.

Chapter 3

IRELAND

What a peculiar set-up this is that I have arrived at. An old established Irish regiment that consists totally of volunteers who are proud of the fact that they are all regular soldiers, and still carry out their duties in the same manner that has been done for many years. Now they suddenly find themselves infiltrated by conscripted fellows from, Birmingham, a large group of Cockneys, and a small contingent from various parts of the country. This is not particularly to their liking, but they now find that their duties are to knock us into shape until we become what they consider to be proper soldiers .

One of the first difficult things was to understand their language, and although it is supposed to be the King's English, it is quite a quaint variety of this that is spoken in Northern Ireland. I quickly realised that it is most important to understand what I am being ordered to do so that life does not become too difficult. I was given my new identity which was that of Rifleman, and the No. 7016755, which was to be my army number for the rest of my active service. I was issued with a paybook which stated that I was entitled to the princely sum of two shillings per day, it also contained all the information about my next of kin, and my last will and testament. This did wonders for my confidence!

Next we were paraded to the Quarter Masters stores to receive the rest of our kit, and that was some revelation. Two of everything. One to wear and, one to wash, so that as the laundry was only done weekly, the one to wear had to last for the whole week. The thing that created the most amusement was the issue of underwear. They were of the type that grandad used to wear long john pants, and vests that buttoned up to the neck and had sleeves. They immediately found there right place in the bottom of the kit bag, only to reappear for kit inspections.

The process of being kitted out, a medical inspection, innoculation and a military style haircut having been completed, I was directed to a first floor barrack room, which had a large stove in the centre and a very highly polished floor. There I was allocated an army bed and a locker. We were then introduced to the Sergeant and a Corporal who were in charge of the twenty-eight recruits that were to become the India Platoon. Early next morning the process of eliminating the need for a brain commenced.

We were instructed that, to the sound of a bugle we would rise from our beds, we would parade for our meals, and we would be back in our beds and put out the lights. It was also made very clear that when you received an order from anyone with stripes or a crown on their arm, you stood quickly to attention and obeyed without question. For anyone with pips on the shoulder, they were to be saluted and addressed as 'sir'. It was made quite clear that recruits were right at the bottom of the order of seniority, but that there was a Field Marshall's baton available to any one of us. Some chance! This was now a complete change in the way of living, the food, and the strict discipline were difficult to become accustomed to, but gradually we began to adapt. In about a couple of weeks it was conceded that we could now dress in a presentable manner and we were allowed out into the small town of Armagh. There was however one proviso, about half of the town was out of

Facing page: *Allowed out for the first time. With the two friends from Birmingham that I met on the train.*

bounds to army personnel unless they were in civilian clothes, and that was the reason that we had been allowed to retain ours purely for this purpose. We had not realised that the Irish problem was so great, as it was something that we had only read about. That had happened in the earlier years, and it came as quite a shock to find that there was such a great divide between the two sides, especially when the two different religions worked so well together during the rest of the week except on Sundays. Great care was taken when the church parades were assembled, to be sure that they headed off in different directions.

We had just about settled down to life in the army in Armagh when the Battalion was moved to the barracks in the grounds of the castle at Ballymena. This was quite an attractive town and surroundings. Life went on much as usual and the process of brain-washing us into soldiers was to continue, so that at any command we obeyed immediately, everything that moved was to be saluted and anything that did not was to be whitewashed or polished.

The ten shillings a week that I got paid did not allow me much high living, but a little relaxation could be found in the YMCA in town at a very reasonable price. I also found that the young lady who sold the stamps, most interesting to have a conversation with, and we enjoyed chatting together even though it was very obvious to me that she had been raised in a very different environment to myself. Quite 'posh' in fact.

One evening while we were talking I mentioned that I must return early to the barracks to prepare for the night patrol that we had to commence at 2200 hrs She said "Be at the gate at a quarter to ten and I will see you there." Promptly on time I went to the gate to find her arriving on a beautiful horse and carrying a container of sandwiches, and a flask of hot coffee laced with a drop of the hard stuff. "These should make things a little more comfortable for you during the night" she remarked and arranged for me to return the flask the following evening. I began to realise that princes or paupers must all look very similar when they are in uniform.

When I returned the flask the following evening, and thanked her for making my night much better than it might have been, she asked me if I was going to the Mayor's Ball in the Town Hall on Saturday evening? The tickets cost more than one week's salary for me so I made some excuse that I would probably be on duty but was not quite sure. She expressed her disappointment and said that a group of her friends, and their partners were all going, she had hoped that I would accompany her and that she had already bought our tickets. I assured her that I would endeavour to be free and let her know the following day.

Having assured her that I had arranged not to be on duty, Saturday night could not come quick]y enough, but what a surprise I got. There were five young ladies, four commissioned officers from the regiment that had been stationed in Ballymena before us, and one 'red arsed' recruit. Me! We had a smashing night at no cost at all to me. The officers had raided their officers' mess bar, and brought a load of booze with them. After my initial concern that I was way out of my league, no one seemed to notice, and if they did they did not make it obvious. The dance had to finish at midnight so we all loaded into the officers' cars and adjourned to the home of my friend. This was some home! And the party went on for some time.

Knowing that I would have problems when returning, a captain in the group accompanied me back to the barracks and safely to my bed. That night I slept like a log only to be awakened in the very early hours, and told to prepare for a trip to the rifle range at Magilligan's Point where we were to be introduced to, and trusted with, live ammunition.for the first time.

It was while we were practising on the rifle range in Magilligan's Point that we realised that things were not going well on the Continent. Those Germans were much better equipped than we had realised, and also a little cleverer, they had totally ignored that great fortification the Magino Line and had gone around or over it. They were now swarming all over Europe driving everything before them, so that it came as no surprise when we were ordered quickly back to barracks to pack up our kit, ready to return to England and travel south to join the Battalion.

This movement was carried out in double quick time, and I soon found myself back in England on the train travelling south and passing through Rugeley Trent Valley station in the night, which was only a good walk from where I lived. Alas there was no opportunity to pay a quick visit home. The trip did however, give me the time to think and to realise that it was not a good idea to put down roots during a war. Yesterday was gone! Tomorrow was another day! And friends that were made, were like passing ships in the night, never to be seen again.

Chapter 4
I JOIN THE LONDON IRISH RIFLES

We eventually arrived at Lowestoft to join the 2nd Battalion of the London Irish rifles. This was the territorial branch in London of the R.U.R. who were stationed in the chalets of a holiday camp that had been established north of the town. We stared with pleasure at the facilities in the chalets, that had been left intact and that we were allocated to. This looked as if it could be quite comfortable. Sprung matresses, feather pillows and white sheets, Great! I joined H company together with a number of my friends, and we were very quickly aware of the captain in charge of the company. He was a very military looking gentleman with a waxed moustache and a very loud voice, that had everyone jumping to attention whenever he was around. He had seen service in the First World War and enjoyed lecturing us on the ways of the Germans, especially the dirty tricks that they could play on one, and that we should be most careful about.

There was however very little time for lectures as the evacuation from Dunkirk had already taken place and everyone was expecting an invasion to happen. Our duty was to defend the coastline to the north of Lowestoft, and each night was spent building defensive positions in sandbags and digging slit trenches, where we would stand, from dusk to dawn. Most of the daytime was taken up in training so that there was no possibility of enjoying the facilities that were available in the holi-

Signature of Soldier _S. Belcher_

Book opens on _____19 . (For the Net Daily Rate
of pay see pages 4 to 9, and Notes thereon.)

If the soldier was in debt on the above date, the amount to be
recovered from the next pay due to him should be stated.

Debt £ _____ s _____

_____ O.C.

Cash Payments.

Date.	Place (If on active Service enter "Field.")	Amount. (State Currency.)	Signature of Officer.
8·3·41	Home	24/.	
7·3·41	do.	30/-	
14·3·41	Field	20/8.	
2·3·41	—	30/-	
26·3·41	—	21/2	
4·4·41	—	30/.	
4·4·41		60 —	
april	P1954	3 9	
18·4·41	Field	10 3	
K.u.A	-	17 6	
2·5·41	-	12 —	
Total Cash Payments to date ...		223 11	

When a soldier is granted leave to England, an entry stating period of furlough is to be made
in second column (i.e., "Place" column).

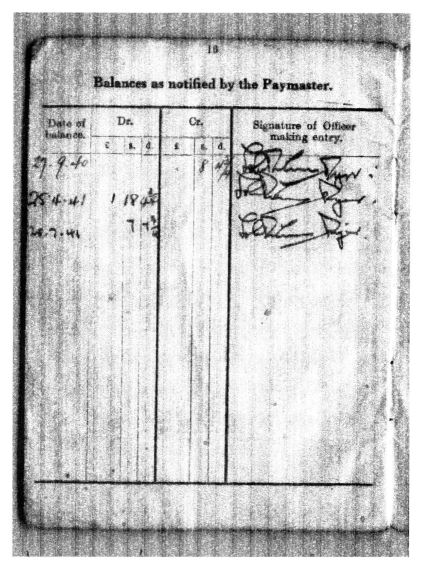

Extract from paybook

day camp.

A lesson that I quickly learned was to get paired up with an Irishman when the duties of digging, or any kind of navvying were to be carried out. There looked like being lots of that, so that Paddy, who had always been rather friendly, quickly became a good buddy. It was strange to realise that the large earthworks that were taking place to the rear of us were hurried efforts by the navy to build positions for their large guns. It was also probably the first time that the Royal Navy had been positioned to the rear of the infantry, but everything seemed to be in rather a turmoil at this time.

There were lots of peculiar movements of troops around the country, and we did not stay in Lowestoft many weeks before we were moved up country to a camp at Knutsford that was in fields behind a small wood, just off the main road.

Our duties were to provide guards on a factory that had gone into the production of aircraft, and was situated a few miles away. That was the general idea but nothing seems to go to plan these days.

After sleeping in one of the tents the first night I reported sick as I was completely lousy with lice, and to my surprise, found many other men also reporting sick with the same complaint. We were taken by truck to the local hospital where we were all washed and cleaned up, only to return to the camp to find it in a proper uproar. The previous occupants of the camp had been men who had returned from the Continent, and this had been a reception camp for them. They had vacated the camp only a few days before we arrived and the whole area was crawling with lice.

It certainly gave us some indication of what the poor devils had gone through in the past few weeks and made us hope that this situation did not arise for us. The hungry little beasts that had been left behind were just dying for another meal, so that when we arrived they really got stuck in and the whole situation became unbearable. It was decided that the whole battalion should be deloused on the Sunday. A couple of very large vans arrived and mobile showers were erected in the next field. Then we were told to parade in the nude, carrying all our clothes packed and ready to go into the vans where they would be treated with a gas. Having done this we proceeded through a gate and were given a blanket, so you can imagine the sight of a whole battalion of nude men in a field for quite a few hours on a Sunday afternoon. "What a picture" "Couldn't tell the officers from the men". "They should have had a different coloured blanket!"

This was of course long before most people had telephones and I was only to learn much later, that when my family knew that I was stationed at Knutsford they decided to hire a car and visit me on the Sunday afternoon. They found the place alright, and arrived at the gate to the camp which was guarded; carrying the goodies that they had brought to surprise me, only to be told that the whole battalion was confined to camp and that it was impossible for me to be allowed out. As no further information was given they were quite disappointed and puzzled as to what was going on. I was quite pleased to learn that they had not been given the real reason, because Mom would not have been very happy to hear that her son was lousy. She had always made sure that I had never been a problem to the "Nit Nurse" at school and I am sure that I would have been getting parcels containing the necessary equipment to prevent it. I did however raise a few smiles when I eventually was able to tell the full story.

Our stay in Knutsford was very short as another camp had to be found immediately. This was at Packington, between Birmingham and Coventry, in the woods again, so that I am getting closer to home with every move.

Here once again the brain washing continued and there seemed to be some confusion over what the role of the battalion was to be. It was at this time that we were instructed that whenever we left the camp we were to carry our rifles and never to be without them as the threat of invasion was very great .

21

I decided that it would be possible for me to make a trip home on Sunday afternoon if I was lucky enough to get a lift. Traffic was very light on the road at this time but I decided to try. I left the camp just before lunch on Sunday and walked down to the crossroads quite close to the camp where the Chester Road which joined up to the Watling Street was a direct route to my home.

A large public house stood at the crossroads where I waited for a lift to come along. The lunch-time session had just finished when a SS Jaguar car open-topped, came roaring off the car park with two happy looking youngish men aboard, and screeched to a halt beside me. "Where are you going?" They shouted. "Cannock" I replied, "If you are prepared to accompany me home, and wait while we have lunch, I will run you to your home," I am told, at which I quickly climbed into the rear seat.

He was certainly a fearless driver and we were soon parked on his drive, where, I was taken inside and the maid was instructed to set an extra place for me at the lunch table. We did not take too long over lunch, and, after he had carried out a few manoeuvres with my rifle on the back lawn he shouted, "Back soon" to his wife, told me to climb aboard and off we shot.

Was this some car? He informed me that he was a test pilot at the local factory that produced fighter planes, and that when he was testing on Monday and he would fly over the camp and do a couple of victory rolls. We were travelling at a pretty good speed along Watling Street when he remarked that the large concrete road blocks that had been set up in case tanks invaded, could be negotiated at 50 miles per hour, and then set about proving it. He roared up to it went into a handbrake skid passing the first half of the block, skidded sideways, and accelerated away as soon as the car was in line to go through, to my great surprise it worked perfectly. Not only did my hair stand on end but there was a real risk that there could have been an awful smell. Actually I really enjoyed the experience and people pay good money to get such thrills. In a very short time we were screeching to a halt outside my mother's shop, where he declined the offer to come in for a "cuppa" and with a wave of the hand he was gone. Another ship that had passed in the night.

I was able to spend a few hours at home, have a good soak in the bath and a chat with the family before "thumbing" my way back to camp before "lights out." On Monday morning I told a few of my colleagues that I had a friend who would be giving us an air display later in the day, and I was so relieved, and proud, when it happened. I am sure that one or two of them wondered what sort of a circle of friends I had? Little did they know, but, how great it feels to bask in unwarranted glory. I was beginning to realise that it does no harm to create impressions. The stay in Packington was very short and we were soon on the move again to Haverfordwest in South Wales.

Here we were to be in billets rather than under canvas and that was a great improvement, and now the army seems to be getting itself in to some sort of order. The change of battalion also brought about a change in my uniform and instead of a normal cap we wore a Caubeen that was rather like a large beret, with a very similar cap badge that was an Irish harp, and at the back of this was a Hackle, which was a bunch of green feathers. The buttons on our uniforms were black and not shiny. This did make us stand out somewhat from the rest of the army and on one occasion when I was travelling on a bus during my first leave, I listened with interest to people behind me who were saying "I think he's Canadian," and she replied, "I think he is Australian". And they both agreed he could be any foreign soldier. It was great when I turned round to say "Hello Vic. How are you?" as he had been my next door neighbour.

I was now getting used to the ways of getting about the country so that at any time it was possible, I could get some time at home. When travelling from the south on a railway ticket to my home town I used to alight at Birmingham New Street where the tickets were collected on the train before it arrived and I was able to retain it, then catch a bus to the edge of town and get a lift home.

When travelling from the north I would endeavour to arrive at Stafford in the early hours, have a cup of tea with the night staff, and get a lift from the G.P.O. van that collected the mail for Cannock who then drove out of the station with me on board and no one ever requested a ticket, so that one railway ticket lasted for many journeys. I was beginning to realise that it can be profitable when using your wits.

We had not been in Haverfordwest very long and were gradually getting used to a dining hall being in the centre of the market, surrounded by stalls that on market days were selling a variety of goods, so that, while the local people were doing their shopping they could be entertained by watching the troops feed ,it was as good as a visit to the zoo for the kids. A most unique situation and must have been just as embarrassing to them as it was to us, but when there is a war on peculiar things tend to happen.

On one Friday I was on the list to do guard at the local jail, a very old dungeon of a place below some civic buildings, where one young Irishman was being held on a charge of attempted murder.

He had never been happy at being transferred to the London Irish Rifles that he considered to be Saturday night soldiers, not in his class, almost at odds with his strong Irish religious beliefs and this had resulted in him constantly being under arrest for misbehaving and committing a variety of offences. His greatest enemy was of course the Provo. sergeant who was a bit of a tyrant, especially when handing out punishment to the ones that were on "jankers". On one occasion when this young Irishman had been scrubbing out the guardroom, he somehow managed to steal a rifle and some ammunition that were kept there for duty, then, dashed to a sandbag enclosure across the square to fire back in the direction of the sergeant everytime he had the nerve to show himself. Eventually, he gave himself up and was now being held in this dungeon awaiting trial for attempted murder.

During my hours of duty we had quite a chat about the whole situation and how he wished he could have remained in the R.U R. He also pointed out that, having acquired the status of a marksman, which was indicated by crossed rifles badge on his arm, it would be quite silly to say that he had attempted to murder the Provo. sergeant, because there was no way that he would have missed him if that had been his intention ,and I thought he had quite a point.

The next morning, preparing to go off duty, I washed and shaved with just one cold water tap over a tub, prior to departing and I was then excused duty for the rest of the day.

Nothing much happened until evening when I decided to go to the pub for a game of darts and a beer and when getting ready realised that my gold signet ring was missing. Thinking about this I realised that the only place I could have lost it was when washing at the jail, so I returned immediately and began to search. There was no sign of it around the tub and even though I immersed my arm and searched in the tub, I did not find it anywhere. So I decided to ask around the guards there, "had any one seen it?" Then a voice from inside the cell shouted "Is this what you are looking for?" And handed me back my ring with the remark "I thought I had better hang on to it for you, rather than hand it to this dishonest lot who would probably have flogged it." l was quietly amused, and very relieved, as it had been a 21st birthday present that I valued quite a lot.

Following this I quickly began to realise that there were much easier duties to be had in the headquarters company that was composed of such specialists as The Band, The Signals, the Transport, the bren gun carriers, the Heavy Mortar Platoon, and the Pioneer Platoon, who all had specialist jobs that they had to carry out, so that they were always too busy to be called for the mundane and boring duties that fell on the

"GOT YER!"

Tank hunters in action

other companies. When I learned that a tank-hunting platoon was to the formed, I quickly let it be known that I would be keen to join such an outfit. As the officer from my platoon was to be in charge I was once again in luck and was one of the 28 men, 4 N.C.Os. and two officers chosen to form the "Tank Hunting Platoon".

We were moved to a billet adjoining the cinema at the top of the hill in the town and began our special training. The first thing was to be issued with a brand new shining bicycle each, none of your dark green army issue about them. Our first duty was to polish them and then to learn to get on to a bicycle by numbers, 1, 2, 3 up, then to proceed along the road in pairs and pedal in time with each other. I had previously been surprised at some of the brain washing that had been done but this was unbelievable and as I have previously said "orders must be obeyed."

We were instructed that our duties were to seek out any tanks that had invaded and destroy them. We collected lots of bottles and were issued with petrol and oil to make them into petrol bombs, to set fire to the tanks. We were also issued with rolls of barbed wire and landmines with which we should construct road blocks, but there was no provision to transport them, so, as the local coal merchant had two 30 hundred-weight Bedford trucks for his business, we gave him a "chitty" to collect his money from the War Office and confiscated one of these trucks. Great! Now we were mobile and could begin our exercises .

Then we were told that tanks had landed and we were to find them, stop them, and destroy them. As soon as the order came that they had landed we were to jump into action. Everything seemed pretty straight forward until the order came, then, when we tried to start the truck the engine would not go. The next hour was spent pushing it up and down the road in order to get it started. I'm afraid I could only see the funny side of this, especially when the day's exercises were called off with the strict orders to get more efficient.

We duly practised mining roads setting up roadblocks making every effort to improve the way we carried out our duties. On one occasion we thought we had found the ideal place to carry out an exercise at a place in the road with a large tree overhanging it. One man could be up in the branches with his petrol bombs, so that when we stopped the tank, he would be sure to hit his target. So this excersise was begun but when he dropped his bombs and they ignited, the flames shot up into the tree and he came hurtling down with his "arse" on fire. One more brilliant result! Undaunted we carried on with our exercises until it was decided that we could set up a show for the top brass of the brigade, and a small stand was built in a position where there were banks each side of the road so that they could sit and watch the action.

The transport department and the pioneers had constructed a mock tank on an old chassis that was to be towed along down this road into the road block where the mines would be set off and the destruction of the tank carried out. As an exercise it went reasonably well and must have impressed the top brass considerably, because within a couple of weeks the tank hunting platoon had been abandoned, and the personnel were split up between the carrier platoon and the mortar platoon. I was fortunate enough to join the carrier platoon and remain in headquarters company.

There were some lighter moments, and possibly funnier ones to be had in Haverfordwest during our stay there, and the concerts that were arranged at the local cinema down by the river on Sunday evenings were well worth going to. We were entertained by our own lads and were surprised at the amount of talent that there was. The band, which looked quite smart in their dark green cloaks and orange kilts, dark green hats with blue hackles, and the drummers with their white gloves that emphasised the tricky movements that they made did not sound at all bad. It was surprising to find what good entertainers we had in the battalion, there were singers, dancers, comedians, and instrumentalists one of whom was named Donald Zec who played the violin. He was very well known later as a columnist on the Mirror newspapers which was his occupation before he joined the forces. At one concert during the time of the bombing on the south of England and London when the battle of Britain was at its worst, he did his imitation of an air raid siren played on his violin on the stage before announcing the number of German planes that had been shot down that day and during the evening of the concert. When he announced that a record number had been destroyed on that particular day, and, even though most of the "turns" had received a good reception, the biggest cheer of the night was heard when we were given that news.

After a few months in Haverfordwest the army seemed to be getting more organised into Brigades and Divisions. We were moved to Malvern in Worcestershire and once again I was within reasonable distance from my home .

Chapter 5

MALVERN

Malvern is a very beautiful place set amongst the hills, and the headquarters company office was in a bungalow in the town. The carrier platoon was billeted at Malvern Wells a couple of miles down the road, in a very large house amongst the "toffs" of the area. As we were separated from the rest of the company, we were allowed our own rations and a cook to look after us. Life soon became quite comfortable, we did maintenance during the day, down where the carriers were parked at the golf course, some driving instruction, and the odd guard duty in the caddies rest room. This was quite a doddle and there was never any shortage of volunteers for this duty.

Just two bren gun carriers had to stand to each night at company headquarters and this was the only duty that was unpopular at the time.

I became a member of the battalion football team as their goalkeeper and my friend Ginger was the captain of the side. We were both also members of the cricket team and life became reasonably pleasant. as the sports ground at the local college was made available for our use.

The guard duty down at the golf course, was a great way of me being able to get home for a weekend as long as my colleagues were in agreement, and there was hardly ever a problem as no one bothered to visit this little outpost. Needless to say I was a regular volunteer for this duty which then allowed

The cricket team at Malvern. My friend, Ginger, is fourth from the left in the back row (standing)

me to get away late on Friday or early on Saturday and return in the early hours of Monday morning, to wake them all up with a "cuppa" and then to report back to the rest of the platoon with the remainder of the guard who had also enjoyed a very relaxed weekend. Naturally there had to be one orderly sergeant who was very conscientious and the weekend he was on duty, I was caught out and brought up on a charge of being absent without leave, to appear on Monday morning in front of the Company Commander.

Arriving early at the Company Office I found complete chaos as the Company Sergeant Major seemed to have lost all the paperwork relating to the charges that were to be brought, and was asking each person when they arrived, "What is your offence?" If the answer was for a minor offence he remarked that he could not bother with that, and instructed them to go away. When I was asked, I said that I had been late on parade but did not make the point that I was two days late. He instructed me to go away and I lost no time setting off back towards our billet when I met the Sergeant who had brought the charge. He was not a very early riser, and he enquired of me "What is going on?" I informed him that it would be better if he did not go to company office as there was chaos over the missing charge sheets, he could have a problem, and that I had been instructed that no charge would be made against me. As my charge was the only one that he was involved with he decided that his best action was to return with me and keep his head down. I was certainly beginning to think that although I am not Irish, the luck of the Irish was on my side.

I was beginning to enjoy life in Malvern; the training was quite interesting, there was a fair amount of relaxation time, and I was able to get home for most of the weekends. The only unfortunate part was that it was the winter time and we were eventually covered with a blanket of snow that prevented lots of the best of the activities. It became quite a dicey business driving a bren gun carrier on snow-packed roads and the slightest oversteer going down a hill could result in the tracks losing their grip and doing an "old time waltz" down the road. We used to get a lot of pleasure from trying to see who could set up this movement and finish nearest to the gate to the billet. Fortunately there was very little other traffic on the road at this time.

One day the whole platoon was instructed to report to the company office to remove all the snow from the bungalow and its surroundings so that it stood out like an oasis in a dessert of white. Everywhere had been cleaned and polished ready for an inspection by the Brigadier that was to be carried out at 1400 hrs. The orderly officer of the day was quite pleased with the result, and ordered an early lunch to be taken so that there would be no problems during the afternoon performance. Unfortunately he had not reckoned with the weather and at one o'clock it started to snow. Calamity!

Caching snowflakes in Malvern

He had a very bright idea and ordered each one of us to take his steel helmet and catch the snow flakes to prevent them from falling on the ground. If you can imagine 30 full grown, fully-trained British soldiers running around catching snow flakes in their helmets, then you have a good picture of what was happening. What a pity that this happened before the days of camcorders I am sure that with this facility this occasion would have been recorded and played to amuse the kids in later years. Well as I have said so often "Orders are orders".

We spent the rest of the winter in Malvern but were soon on the move again and having heard of the impending move, I decided to have the last weekend at home, without permission of course and got away early on Friday night, not having bothered to read Battalion orders. That was a great mistake as I was down to play in goal for the Battalion football team against the

32

South Wales Borders on the Malvern College ground. It was of course impossible for me not to be posted as being absent without leave this time, and on Monday I was brought once again before the Commanding Officer and given seven days confined to barracks.

Calamity. Calamity.

Well not quite, as we were to move next day, the whole battalion was to move by road to Sussex, this was to be also used as an exercise in moving a large number of troops. So being a carrier driver, that is what I did for the next few days, and when we arrived in Eastergate in West Sussex, my time of C.B. was finished, before it was even started. The luck still seemed to be with me.

Chapter 6

SUMMER IN SUSSEX

We arrived in Eastergate in West Sussex in the spring hoping for a good summer. This was far better than we had expected and we were really looking forward to the next few months. The carrier platoon was billeted in a pair of semi-detached brand new dwellings that had not quite been completed, in that the kitchens and bathrooms had not been fitted, and no painting had taken place. But they were really good billets and as they also had an attached garage each we were able to use one as a dining room. Once again being detached from the company, we had all our own catering facilities and lived rather well.

The bren gun carriers were garaged about three hundred yards away behind a bungalow that was used for platoon headquarters, at the rear of which was a small gravel quarry now unused, where we could parade and maintain our vehicles and motorcycles. It was quite a good set-up and we could amble up and down from the billets, until one day the sergeant decided that we were getting too relaxed in our ways.

Attached to us was a mechanic from the R.A.S.C. in charge of the maintenance of all the vehicles, even though at the time he was only a lance corporal. He was the most brilliant mechanic that I have ever met and could tell by the sound of an engine exactly what, if anything, was wrong with it. He had the most novel way of testing a plug by holding it and letting

Above: *The author with Walcot and Corporal Charnock in their bren gun carrier at Eastergate.*
Below: *Hank at the wheel of his bren gun carrier at the gravel quarry Eastergate.*

the spark cross from his finger nail to any metal part of the vehicle, or at times he would grab you by the hand and give you the most awful shock which did not seem to affect him in any way . He was quite the most liked fellow amongst us, as we could take all our problems to him and he would have them resolved in no time at all. Unfortunately he did not welcome the other duties of being a soldier so that when this sergeant decided that we should march to and from the billets he did not join in, and the Sergeant immediately brought him on a charge. When he was brought before the C.O. he made an application for a transfer back to his own company and this was granted much to our disgust. We used to make it very plain to this highly efficient Sergeant. What a prat!

It was sometime later that we next saw this mechanic with two pips on his shoulder and the cleanest pair of hands he had had for years. He informed us that he had been sent on an Officers Training course which he had passed with flying colours, so that his small transgression of not wanting to march with us had done him a great favour. Some promotions had always been a mystery to me. But this was one that I agreed with entirely.

Things were going along very nicely and to add a bit of variety to my work, I volunteered at times to do the duties of the clerk in the office or of the technical storeman in the store for the spare parts for the vehicles. Both jobs had quite a different interest and were reasonably easily done so that I enjoyed the variety of the work during the time that the regular occupants of the posts were on leave or had to go on a course.

We eventually moved on to the Royal Drive to Goodwood racecourse and were once again under canvas. This was not too bad and the only problem we had there was the fact that we were under chestnut trees, and were plagued with rats, until we decided to have a day's sport catching them. We did this by extending our exhaust pipes into their holes until they all came out staggering and were easy to dispose of, so that we eventually finished up with at least two barrow loads, Ah well! it was a diversion from the usual run of things

Another diversion came from the usual duties when it was decided to erect steel tubular scaffolding as a tank defence along the whole of the South Coast line. We had to start at Selsey Bill and work down towards Brighton. It was great being on the beach in the sunshine on the Sussex coast and this was one of the better duties that we had to perform, almost like being back on a building site and more a relaxation than a duty as lots of our time was also spent swimming in the sea. Like all good things, it was quickly completed and life took on its normal duties of maintenance, training, driving instruction and the more mundane things that had to be carried out.

I was having a lazy Sunday morning when I was informed that I had volunteered to form the crew of a small canvas sided invasion boat that was to race down the river Arun to the mouth of the river by the Littlehampton golf club house, which was to be the finishing line. This came about because of a bet that had been made between some of the officers in their search for something different to pass away a dull Sunday. We loaded into a truck and were taken to the starting point way up the river beyond Arundel and there were about eight of these craft with four men to paddle, two each side and the officer in charge sitting at the rear and steering. For the next few hours we were on one knee paddling like mad trying to get into the current as much as possible and having a rare old tussle with each other. As we passed under the bridge at Arundel the river was running rather fast and we got on a pretty good rate of knots. Then, having won the race, we were all feeling pretty knackered when we arrived at the finishing line and were quite incapable of turning for the shore. We were being swept out to sea when a boat came out and towed us back to the finishing post where we were lifted from our boat, still stuck in the kneeling position and our limbs massaged back into use so that we could get to the bar of the golf club. The first two pints never touched the sides, especially as they were already paid for.

It is at times like this that the comradeship between the men is so apparent and it is very seldom that there are any arguments at all — everyone seems to enjoy each other's company so that the one thing that has been accomplished over the last month's is that if, and when, we become dependent on each other in action, that will not be a problem at all.

We eventually went back into billets and the carrier platoon were stationed in a hotel at the most extreme point of Selsey Bill. At this time I was doing relief duty for the clerk. The order came through that all clerks had to be trade tested that day and that I had to go to brigade headquarters and take a test. Even though I protested that I was already tested as a driver mechanic and that the regular clerk was away on leave, this did not make any difference and the test had to be done. It was so simple that it was no problem to pass, and there was then an increase in my pay much to the disgust of the regular clerk when he returned from leave.

Once again when you get a order, you obey, and ask questions afterwards, but it does make you think where on earth some of these orders come from.

The summer that we had spent in West Sussex had been so good, and when I thought about it, I doubt if I could ever have spent a whole summer on or around the south coast, the seaside towns, the sandy/pebbly beaches, swimming in the sea, touring on the south downs, and enjoying all these pleasures with a lot of comrades that it was so good to be with. Even when carrying out the duties that involved doing evening patrols or guard duties, there was the unique entertainment of listening to the nightingale which was a pleasure never experienced before and never to be forgotten. It's a hard life in the army, and now at two shillings and sixpence a day! I shall be sorry to leave Sussex, but inevitably that was getting very iminent.

We decided to have an evening out at a club in Selsey Bill on the night before we were to move to a destination which was unknown to us at the time, and it was early in the morning

Our motorcycle section at Eastergate. Our brilliant mechanic is the second from the right.

when I arrived worse for wear, back to the billets only to find that everyone was lining up ready for off. One of my mates had already packed my kit and loaded it aboard the bren gun carrier so that I was able to climb into the back, get my head down, and have a good kip — not really knowing much about what was happening, only to wake up hours later to find myself well on the way to the borders of Norfolk and Suffolk near to Brandon.

Chapter 7

NORFOLK

It seems strange that our battalion "flits" around the country and seems to serve no particular purpose, especially when other battalions are getting sent to the Middle and the Far East, but this is down to the powers that be, and I can only consider that it is part of my good fortune to be a member of the London Irish Rifles. It is surprising how it gets to you, and you eventually become proud of the regiment that you serve.

The make up of the platoon changed slightly from time to time, the ambitious ones being promoted and transferred to the infantry companies, new faces brought in to take their places, quickly integrated into the ways of our platoon and we became like one large family.

We became aware of the peculiarities of our officers and N.C.O.s and were able to cope with them pretty well. I remember on one occasion, on a Sunday afternoon when we were lazing on our beds and, in came our Commanding Officer with the Orderly Sergeant shouting the order "Stand by your beds". Everybody stood to attention just as they were, and an inspection was carried out by the officer who had had a good liquid Sunday lunch. One Cockney Lance Corporal named Crisp, who was about six feet tall and weighed about 8 and a half stone stood there in his real greasy caubeen and Hackle on his head, white P.T. vest, blue P.T. shorts, gaiters, and boots. How on earth he was dressed in this fashion is difficult to under stand but when they reached him they stopped in amazement with the following remark "Crirrrsp! Crrirrrsp! You're like a wet dream in Technicolour." The whole room burst into gales of laughter but were just able to hear the Sargeant cry out "stand easy! Fall out!" This is typical of things that used to happen occasionally, carried out by officers to annoy other ranks, that were having a lazy afternoon or, most probably to give them a laugh when they recounted it in the mess, but we could take these things in our stride and at times also enjoyed the fun of the occasion.

Unfortunately this particular officer was keen to join the army air force to pilot the Lysander spotter planes that were used, and around this time he was successful in his request, so that he left us. This was a great pity as he was a very popular guy. The Lieutenant who had been in charge of the tank hunting platoon and who was second in command was now promoted to captain and became commander of the carrier platoon. There were lots of promotions knocking about as other people left to different duties but we were so comfortable in our roles that we had no ambitions. However my friend "Fishy" looked on orders one day and saw that he had been promoted to Lance Corporal. "Great! That is another seven days leave", and in no time at all after this promotion, he went missing for a week. As soon as he returned he was charged with being A.W.O.L. and received the obvious punishment for his offence, reduced to the ranks so that he returned to the situation that he enjoyed, and back with his mates.

It was something of a shock to see the camp that we arrived at in Norfolk, and it can best be described by the remark of one Cockney lad when he opened the door of the Nissan hut on the first morning. "Cor Blimey!" he cried "There is nothing art here but great big fields and Christmas trees" and that is a fair description of the area in which we were stationed. Unfortunately, a lot of the larger open areas were planted with sugar beet which was now ready for harvesting and, guess what? The infantry companies used to be shipped out daily into fields to help the land army girls to cut sugar beet. What a job, although I suspect that at times there were some rewards, thank goodness we were able to avoid this work. And for us life went on much as usual.

There was not much chance of getting home from this out of the way posting and train journeys across country were the slowest that you could imagine, making the journey home difficult, so that I resigned myself to making the most of what was available locally. The "Passion" truck which left every evening at 6pm was only allowed to travel 20 miles. As the nearest town, which was King's Lynn was about twenty two miles away, the bus used to park up and everyone had to walk the remainder. I did not use this facility and often walked to a local village for a drink, which sometimes was quite a distance. It was not uncommon at this time for all bicycles to be collected from near to the camp especially on Monday monnings and taken to the nearest police station to be called for by their owners. This situation never seemed to result in any further action being taken which was considered a very civilised way of behaving.

Most of the villages had a troupe of Home Guard who welcomed the use of a bren gun carrier or two to act as the enemy for their exercises on Sunday monning, and we soon realised the benefit of volunteering for this job. The headquarters for them were usually at the local pub and after the exercises were carried out where they ambushed us as we tried to enter their village using stirrup pumps to represent machine guns, sacks of whitening to represent Grenades and hiding in the most unusual places. They were usually successful in repelling the enemy just before opening time when we all adjourned to the bar to discuss their tactics and to receive their generosity. It was generally a very good morning that had been totally enjoyed by all.

Life was beginning to get rather boring much the same every day and in the evening the constant drone from the bombers that occupied the airfields all around us, going off in the early evening fully loaded and having great difficulty in getting their aircraft up over the trees when setting off to bomb the Continent, then in the early hours, returning back to base. There seemed to be little point in what we were doing and it was getting to the stage where we were hoping that more exciting things were to happen, when we were informed that we were to be moved to Scotland to become part of the Irish Brigade in the 1st Army.

Chapter 8
NORTH OF THE BORDER

The whole battalion moved to the county of Ayrshire in Scotland, near to the mining villages of Auchinleck and Cumnock, where we were to form The Irish Brigade with the Inniskillins who were affectionately known as the "Skins", the Irish Fusiliers who were affectionately known as the Fogs", and the 2nd Battalion of the London Irish Rifles. This Brigade was then to become part of the 6th armoured division that was forming part of the new 1st army now being assembled in Scotland.

It was obvious immediately upon our arrival in Scotland that things were to be quite different in the future. The comfortable times that we had been having recently were quickly coming to an end. We had also the problem of understanding the local people. So that when the local lads came up with the shouts "Wull yer gei us a hurrl on yerr wee tarnk misterr" or if the girls in the NAFFI said "lf ye can no ge in a strraight line ye'll no ge serrrved". We really thought we had landed in a foreign country. But we soon got used to them and found them to be quite opposite to the mean people that the Scots were supposed to be, and they were the most generous of people. They went out of their way to do us favours and would go without themselves to provide us with little extras. It was quite a revelation to us, and we were made more welcome there than we had been made anywhere else in the country.

The change soon began to take effect and the old divisional signs were all removed from the vehicles, which was a little sad saying goodbye to the Bow Bells, and the sign of the Iron Fist of the 6th Armoured division taking its place on our sleeves and on all of our vehicles. We were once again under canvas but this time it was obviously with a purpose, so that all the equipment, such as cooking and dining, storing facilities offices, bathing and toilet, in fact all our needs for active service were in position so that we could get accustomed to these conditions, The job of co-ordinating us into a real army was now beginning.

Not only was the efficiency going to be brought up to a much higher standard but the fitness was also to receive "the treatment" for instance the early morning cross country run that was introduced before breakfast, covered quite a few miles, and in this country a few miles entails crossing a rather shallow river quite a number of times. It is no joke at some time between 6 and 7 am to be dashing around in and out of freezing cold water for as least 1 hour per day. But the hot showers were always working pretty well, even though they were only surrounded by canvas and we were soon ready for breakfast.

Very soon the business of bringing all the equipment and vehicles up to standard was begun and we were to receive a whole new fleet of bren gun carriers that needed to have their engines run-in ready for service. For this purpose "Fishy", "Hank," and myself, were detailed to report every morning for rations to take out with us as we would be driving all day, to wherever the fancy took us. We really enjoyed this assignment. During the next few weeks we must have covered a vast area of Scotland around Glasgow, until every one of the new vehicles had been run in and had all their oil changed so that they were now ready for service. We quickly realised that the place to stop for lunch was outside any promising-looking house which invariably came up with the invitation to "come inside for drinks",or at times appeared with a tray loaded down with goodies. At least we had retained the art of getting about without a stick. "Hank" was a past master at this and was an artist at picking the right places and the right people.

The exercise of getting all the vehicles, kit, and materials up to the highest standard continued, and at the same time any personnel who were not quite up to standard were given attention to put things in order and if this was not possible they were to be returned to the regimental headquarters. Of the personnel who arrived to take the place of the ones that had had to depart, two that I remember well were, "Spud" Murphy and "Pedlar" Palmer. Spud was a newsagent and tobacconist in his normal life and had access to unlimited amounts of tobacco so that his pipe was never out unless he was asleep. He even kept it going when he was on parade and it disappeared up his sleeve between taking a puff. He was quite a character and the one thing that he liked most was fishing, so that to be stationed amongst the Scottish rivers was his ideal and most of his spare time was spent practising casting on the river. His kit bag contained waders, gaffs, flies, boxes of hooks — all fisherman's equipment. He even bought himself a bicycle so that he could get down to the best parts of the river quicker in the evenings. On one occasion he was in trouble because the engine of his carrier had seized up, and he was brought up before the C.O. on a charge of neglecting his maintenance. This went on for some time and meant that he had to pay a number of visits to company office which did not please him at all because, not only did it take up good fishing time, it meant that he must get all dressed up properly for the occasion. This was the part that he really hated, so in despair he stopped the proceedings on one visit and said to the C.O. "What is the cost of a new engine? If you will find out, get one fitted and give me the bill, I will see that it is paid so that we can get back to normal living". The C.O. was so taken aback at this suggestion that he dismissed the charge, and ordered the report to say that there was a fault with the original engine. This was quite typical of "Spud" anything for an easy life and

46

nothing to interfere with his favourite hobby.

After some time of getting re-organised it was decided that a large exercise, using the whole of the 1st Army over a very large area of Scotland should take place lasting for 10 days. It was quite a revelation to see so much military action taking place and unfortunately there were lots of casualties and accidents, almost as if it was the real thing.

Battalions and companies were moving into action. Tanks and artillery guns were brought up in support, all of it being monitored by officers who were to say what results would have been brought about by various actions. How many men would have been killed or captured, and a general report on the whole of the exercise. We were at one time stationed in a village awaiting further orders and needed to stop overnight. "Hank"quickly found the local baker and decided that we should park the bren gun carriers in his yard. This was great thinking on his part, and we quickly realised the variety of cakes, buns, and other goodies, that are made in a country bakery and that we were lucky to sample. His ingenuity was unbelievable. At the end of the exercise everybody returned to their camps and the top brass held a conference to discuss the merits of the whole thing.

We were about threequarters of the way through the excersise when Fishy sprained an ankle and it was decided that he should be taken back to camp. We could use a motorcycle and sidecar for this purpose, and that I should accompany Fishy to help him, and Hank should drive the motorcycle so that he could return to the exercise. We lost no time in getting away and had about 25 miles to travel back to the camp. This we did and were flying round the bends and having a rare old time. Those old Norton combination motor cycles were a peculiar vehicle — just a box for a sidecar, but when the drive to the sidecar wheel was engaged, they could only be driven in a straight line. This was only for use on a roughtrack. In no time at all we were entering the track down to camp and had to turn right over a depression in the ground, off the track, and up to our tent. It was at this time that the motorcycle and the sidecar parted company. Fishy in the sidecar continued down the track for a few yards while we turned up the field. We all realised how fortunate we had been for this to happen when it did, and not when we were scorching round the bends driving back. I was convinced that my good luck run remains intact. The days until they all returned to camp were quite a rest from the normal and we made the most of them, Fishy getting well back on the road to recovery. The next day we were very surprised to see "Big Mac", who had gone on leave about nine months ago, and not been seen or heard of since, come strolling down the drive, kitbag on his shoulder and dressed good enough for inspection just as if everything was normal. He was a hell of a fellow, over six feet tall and fourteen stones at least. He said that he had got fed up with trying to keep one step ahead of the redcaps, and scrounging for his food and keep, so that he had decided to return. He just could not believe it, that on the day he returned, the battalion was "out". As nobody seemed to be very interested, we decided that he could "kip" down with us and await their return. This gave him a few days to get used to the life again before the inevitable punishment of a spell in a detention camp, which he served before he returned to us.

Shortly after the exercise was over a number of us were in the NAAFI tent where a bit of foolery was going on, when someone decided to blow up a French letter like a balloon, then allow it to fly off. This eventually was helped round and round the NAAFI for some time, and must have lost its interest when nobody seemed to bother what had happened to it, until there was a cry from one of the girls round at the rear where the crocks were washed up. Apparently it had fallen into one of the cups and found its way into the kitchen area and then all hell let loose. It was immediately reported to the commanding officer, who decided that until the culprit for this terrible offence was found, and punished, the whole Battalion should be confined to camp.

Later that day I was told to report to company office, where I was informed to pack my kit so that I could leave the next morning for one month's leave. This seemed unbelievable but farmers could request the release of former employees to help with their harvest, and, the farmer who had been kind enough to find my father some work, decided that it would be a good wheeze if he could get away with it by requesting my helping him, so he had applied and been successful. That is the reason that on the morning that the whole battalion was confined to camp, I set off with a railway warrant in my pocket and my kit on my shoulder to spend one month at home.

During the time that I was away, preparations for some sort of action was really speeding up and it was decided that King George 6th should visit the Brigade. I can't say that I minded missing that parade. All that "spit and polish".

Chapter 9

PREPARING FOR ACTION

Great! I'm free for a month, no revallie, no early morning cross country run through the river, no need to shave every day, and the only discipline was my own. I could not believe it, but the realisation that I was expected to work on the farm removed a little bit of the shine from the ginger bread. Just to be away from the battalion was great, but the one big shock was how much I had got out of the habit of, and the capability of doing manual work. It was pretty hard going, mowing right around fields with a scythe to allow the binder access to start cutting, and this soon took its toll, so that all the muscles that I had developed in the P.T. sessions soon began to ache, and for the first few days I was very stiff, until it gradually wore off. The days of the combined harvester had not yet arrived so that all the jobs were manual, stacking the stooks to dry, then loading onto carts, then unloading into Dutch barns, or making new ricks in the fields, was all arm and wrist work that took sometime to get used to. On the third or fourth morning at home, a letter arrived from Fishy, and this was a great surprise as he was not known for writing letters, and probably is better known for not writing. He told me that he and Bartlett, had decided that they should clear up the confusion that had kept them all confined to barracks, by seeking an appointment with the commanding officer to explain that there were many men involved, but no one person was responsible for the result of their actions. They were hoping that he would understand. And as Fishy said, "He surely did — so that Bartlett and I have volunteered for seven days CB, which we are now serving" and that this has given him time to write to me. It was a very good lesson in the truth of the advice "never volunteer for anything."

It was great to be amongst my family and all the comforts of home, such as sprung mattress, sheets on the bed and meeting lots of friends for a drink down at the local. But just as I was really getting used to it, the month was over. I had to return to Scotland, and though it seems rather a strange thing to say, I rather enjoyed meeting up with all the lads again.

I had quickly got back in to the way of things, when my right wrist became quite painful and started to swell up, it also creaked like an old door-hinge whenever I used it, so that I reported sick, and was sent by the M.O. with my small kit to the local hospital at Ballochmylle. The doctor diagnosed Teno synovitis and he decided that I could stay in hospital to give it complete rest for three weeks. This really was magic, feeling fine myself, doing nothing at all, and being waited on by the smashing nurses. These Scottish girls certainly know how to treat a patient and were great company.

Our ward was all army chaps with a variety of complaints, and one that I recall was on the verge of becoming a monk when he had opted to join the forces, so he was very naive in the ways of some of the nurses, who really gave him a torrid time, especially if they were on night duty, when they would dive into his bed and get him very excited. I wish I could have got a large wager that he did not go into a monastery if he survived the war. He was already beginning to enjoy his stay in hospital. The other character was Jack the Red Cap who had been in the hospital since the ten week exercise when he was on M.C. patrols.

One night when escorting a convoy of trucks he met with an accident and he swore that he was in collision with one truck, the next three, seeing that he was a red cap, had not bothered to avoid him in any way at all, but had just continued over the bump. The injuries that he had suffered were pretty terrible, one thigh and two legs broken, internal injuries, a fractured skull — so that when he had arrived in hospital he was in a very poor state. The nurses on the ward were all proud of the way that they had nursed him back to reasonable health and he was their favourite patient. During his stay in the hospital he had taken to writing short stories, and some of the nurses were featured in them to their great pleasure.

We enjoyed a lot of conversations together, and soon became very friendly, so that when he was able to get around on two crutches, I was able to accompany him down to the canteen. He was very anxious to get out for a change so that a nurse who lives in the local village agreed, that if he was allowed out he could have lunch with them. The doctor agreed that he would be allowed out only if I promised to look after and accompany him, so that this was the arrangement.

It was a slow job getting down to the gate to catch the local bus to the village but we made it and were made very welcome by the family of the nurse, who put on a smashing lunch. At opening time her father invited us to accompany him for a drink, and we lost no time in agreeing, but as we were wearing hospital blue uniform we were not allowed into public houses and had to drink in the kitchen rather than the bar. This was not much of a deterrent and the Scottish way of drinking is a whisky and a chaser every round, this soon took its toll and we were both feeling the worse for wear when it was time to catch the bus to get us back to the hospital by eight o'clock. We managed to board with a bit of difficulty and very soon we were being dropped off at the main gate. It was impossible for Jack to manage the distance up the main drive on his crutches, so that I decided to carry him, he climbed on to my back with two crutches across my chest. The only way we could make progress was by a slow jog to the ward door which we surprisingly made without mishap. The whole of the day staff had remained on duty awaiting their special patient to return from his first trip out in months. When I stood him up by the ward door, opened it and pointed to his bed saying "You can make it mate". He 'clonked' his way right to the edge of the bed before falling forward on to it, and 'spilling' the lot all over the bed. There was a little rush to assist him, change his bed, and make him very comfortable, before they angrily turned to me saying that I should be ashamed for getting him into such a state. After a couple of aspirins, the following morning Jack assured me that he had had a really good day out and thanked me.

It was not long after this that I was returned to the battalion to continue my duties but unfortunately within a very short time, the wrist became a problem once again and I reported to the M.O. who was instructing me what to do to get treatment at the hospital, when I assured him that having recently been there, I knew the procedure. Whereupon he decided that probably a change would be better, and that he would send me to a hospital in Glasgow. Me and my big mouth! If I had kept quiet I should have once again been back in Ballochmyle hospital.

I reported to the hospital in Glasgow where they decided that they would put my arm in plaster from the elbow to the base of my fingers, and that way it would rest the best, until it was recovered. This was done and I was returned to my billet and excused all duties. I spent most of my time in the days following helping as "bookies" runner, getting a few beers in the pubs where I collected a few bets, and getting invited into people's houses for a meal. Everyone was so sympathetic for this chap who had his arm in a sling and had obviously been injured. I did not go out of my way to enlighten them. Well, why spoil a good thing?

Meanwhile things were happening rather quickly and it was obvious that shortly the battalion would be going abroad. The vehicles had all been delivered to the docks and loaded aboard ships and I was sent to join the "odds and sods" that were to be sent back to the depot in Northern Ireland. Thinking about this I wondered whether once again I had been in luck, but two days before we were to leave a truck arrived, and the driver asked where my kit was? He had to load up and take me back to the carrier platoon. This was quite a surprise as I still had my arm in plaster and a sling, but on arrival the captain called me into the office and said that he had got special permission from the battalion Commander for me to rejoin the platoon. He said that he realised that I would not wish to be parted from all my comrades and that as we had spent such a long time together preparing for this, that I would want to be part of the action. Nice Man!

The whole battalion was lined up on the station yard two days later waiting to board the train for the King George V docks in Glasgow where the largest convoy ever to leave the country was being assembled. We were to board the ship The Duchess of Athlone "the drunken Duchess" and an N.C.O. was detailed to carry my kit aboard the train and to attend to it when we got to the dock, so that I was strolling along on my own like a very special person when a telegraph boy came riding into the railway yard with a telegram, and guess what! It was for me from my sister and said "its a boy!"

I began to wonder whether my good luck had begun to change as we were informed that there was to be an invasion of North Africa from the Algiers area, and the 1st Army were to carry it out so that they would close the back door of the desert to the Germans who were retreating from the advancing troops there. The trip on the boat was fairly uneventful for the first eight days, we proceeded half way across the Atlantic to the North of Ireland before turning around to head back to the Straits of Gibraltar. During the whole of this time I still had my arm in a sling and was being waited upon, until the day before we were due to leave, when I saw the ship's doctor to have the plaster removed.

This became quite an operation as he had not got the facilities, never having had to carry patients like this before, so we struggled with a small hacksaw and large scissors until it was eventually hacked away and I found that I had very little use in that wrist. He bound it up tight with a large elastic plaster and said it would probably be OK in a few days. The next day, having slipped through the Straits under the cover of darkness, we arrived at Algiers where a couple of boats had been sunk in the harbour but we were fortunately able to dock and disembark. Having lost my sling and plaster I got all my kit back and resumed all my usual duties, but with a little difficulty. Favours all finished! We were marched to a large field on the edge of town, given a two man bivouac and were instructed that we were to stay there for that night. But as soon as we arrived it started to pour with rain and we became very disillusioned with our first impression of the African weather.

This was the first time that I began to think that all the luck I had enjoyed was beginning to desert me at last. But the next morning after a very miserable night the sun came up and things once again began to look much brighter.

Chapter 10

North Africa

We were informed that as our transport had been shipped further along the coast we would be staying for a few days near to the town of Algiers, until we could be transported by train to collect our vehicles. This meant that we had a short time to get accustomed to the weather, the country, and the people. These things were all such a surprise to us, such as warm days, cold nights, oranges and olives growing on trees in a very fertile area, but the treatment of the natives by the French settlers was a proper shock. The restrictions placed upon them were pretty awful which annoyed some of the lads especially when the shoe-shine boys, who used to earn a few francs by polishing our boots and were more of a novelty than a nuisance, were chased by the police and if caught, physically punished.

On one occasion when two policemen were being pretty rough to a few of these boys, "Big Mac" grabbed them, one in each hand, lifted them up, and banged them together. Then with a kick up the arse, they were the ones to be glad to run away. As a result we had shiny boots for the rest of our stay.

The Yanks who had also landed a small force for their first introduction to land warfare were mostly settled down in the town, and another brand new experience was to see them queuing up to get into the brothels. That certainly was a first!

It was about a week before we moved on and my wrist had returned to normal. We were loaded into wagons on the railway to go to pick up the bren gun carriers. As we passed through a small station on the journey, there were boxes of oranges and dates awaiting despatch on the platform, and as these trains did not move very fast their numbers were considerably reduced as we passed through. The novelty of so much fruit being available soon wore off.

The Battalion eventually collected all their equipment and formed up into a large convoy to commence the long journey over the Atlas mountains towards Tunisia. We were issued with enough boxes of "compo" rations for the journey.

This was a new method of feeding the troops on active service, 1 box of rations for 14 men for one day or one man for 14 days and everything was split up into breakfast of tinned bacon and two other meals in tins, together with biscuits, dried milk, tea, sugar, cigarettes, and even toilet paper. Clipped to some of the tins was the smallest most efficient tin-opener that I had ever seen. This was one of the most successful innovations to army life in the field. We soon developed a very easy way of preparing a hot meal. An empty petrol can with the top removed was half filled with sand, which was soaked with petrol and set alight. Into another petrol can half full of water went the tins that we required, this took a fairly short time for them to be quite hot enough to eat and it was always a very good idea to open them underneath a cloth. It was great to get hot meals and especially the treacle "pud" that was the favourite of most of the lads, the only thing that we missed was fresh bread. The one improvement that I thought of quite a few times later on, was that for troops who were in action for the first time, the supply of "bog roll" was quite inadequate.

The next point, for replacing our supply of food and fuel was on the outskirts of Constantine, and the sight of this town as we drove in, was the most beautiful view that I have seen. Built up the very steep sides of a deep valley with a long bridge as a centrepiece, it was certainly something to remember. The convoy had to drive around a large sports field that was stacked with supplies, load up with rations and petrol, and then form into a very slow moving convoy until the whole lot had been supplied and were ready for the rest of the journey. As we moved along at about a couple of hundred yards at a time, this took up a few hours during which the local young ladies tagged along, much to the pleasure of the lads. One very beautiful French girl must have walked quite a few miles with us, but as we only had enough French to request food or water, and she had little or no English, it was difficult trying to converse, but we did our best with an "impeccable"" sign language, that left nothing in doubt. A bright interlude. Another ship in the night.

The next stage of the journey was over the mountains and was pretty hairy driving, especially in a bren gun carrier. The road at times seemed to be precariously ledged on the side of the mountain with a deep ravine on the other side. Just how difficult it was, was very evident from the number of vehicles that were wrecked at the bottom of the ravine. It was much more difficult for tracked vehicles as they tend to slide easily if the surface of the road is smooth. We were pretty lucky and did not lose a vehicle until we were back on more level going, and a carrier went off the road and into the clinging mud that this ground turns into after rain. It is the most clinging mud that is so difficult to remove, and the clutch on the carrier burnt out so that it had to be abandoned. This did not seem to be a great problem and another vehicle was ordered and that was the first lesson in the difference of being on active service where things could now be written off as lost in action.

The most noticeable thing happening as we got nearer to the action zone, was the difference in the mood of the men. Everything became a little more serious, a sort of apprehension seemed to be creeping in, the crafty deviation slowly disappeared and we all gradually seemed to get closer together, always ready to give a hand if needed, as if in a clear anticipation of what would be needed soon.

We were getting very near to where we should be in contact

with the German forces when the first casualty for the battalion ocurred. One of the lads who was a bit of a John Wayne type of a fellow, enjoyed walking around with bags of ammunition in his pouches. His rifle always loaded, hand grenades hanging from his belt and a couple of personnel mines also hanging at his rear. This became a tragic mistake because as he was walking over some rocky ground he stepped on to a sloping rock and fell backwards on to the mines. This was a great shock, especially to his close friends in our platoon, and it was a hard but very serious lesson to us all that war is very dangerous and your own weapons should be treated with the utmost care and respect. Another incident that emphasised the difference from everything that we had learned over the years in England, and the real thing, was when the medical officer came to pronounce him dead and the padre did his duty at the burial, marking the spot so that he could be "Called for later" to be moved to a permanent place. This done we moved on again, another ship had passed not to be completely forgotten, but a lesson quickly learned.

The dash to try to secure the port of Tunis by Christmas had been terribly delayed by the very bad weather turning the ground into a quagmire, and so we found that we were to be situated on the foothills around the Bou Arada Plain with the Jerries in close proximity. As their lines of communication to Southern Italy were so much shorter they had been able to establish themselves to a line some 50 or so miles from the port, so that now, at last, this was the real thing, as we soon realised when the Stuka dive bombers quickly found our convoy arriving and carried out what they probably thought was a welcoming party. They came swooping down from the sky like a hawk descending on a sparrow, but with sirens blaring, machine guns blasting, and then bombs dropping. Even the slowest man becomes a sprinter and it is possible to get much closer to the ground than you have ever imagined could be done.

As we were still only a small force we were spread pretty

Reprinted from DAILY TELEGRAPH, MAY 1943

" BOU ARADA "

"The bloodiest single day battle of the Tunisian Campaign."

On January 20 the London Irish started what was the bloodiest single-day battle of the whole campaign. Crossing the Bou Arada Plain in daylight, they took up position behind the Inniskillings, who had been having a tough encounter with the Hermann Goering Regiment on Two-Tree Hill.

In moonlight, in a cleft in the rocks, the commanding officer gave his orders for the battalion to attack. It was met with heavy fire.

But the attack went on and the enemy was driven back from one of his strong points. The initial attack had been very costly. Daylight brought a plastering of the London Irish positions by heavy German artillery and mortars and an attack by 21 dive-bombers. But the London Irish held on.

Attack followed counter-attack, and at midnight the enemy brought up tanks, including the "Tiger" Mark VI, as well as infantry. They came in behind the London Irish, sweeping the ground with fire.

Inevitably there were many casualties, and a battalion of Guards was brought in to relieve the London Irish. The German thrust to the Goubellat-Bou Arada road was for the time being finished, and the London Irish had won a battle honour which was on a par with the great effort at the battle of Loos in the last war.

thinly along our battle line and settled into these positions to await our orders.

The tactical manoeuvres and the general reports of this phase of the war have been recorded in quite a few places, so that I do not intend to dwell upon this, only to recall the incidents that were considered too minor to be recorded. But they are so well remembered by all the lads that were there.

In the very early days, most of the action was to carry out patrols to try to find out the position and strength of the enemy and it was on a very damp December day that I was instructed to parade with six other men to accompany the second in command on such a patrol, to find a suitable position in a small mosque on the top of a hill for an Observation Post. As we prepared and blacked up our faces we were lectured by the Officer that it was just an observation patrol and on no account were we to engage the enemy if we encountered them. His remarks were "because if they catch you they will cut your f——g throats". This did wonders for our morale even before we started out. The patrol went reasonably well until we were returning in the early hours and had to cross a very muddy area of the plain. It appeared as if each leg weighed a hundred-weight with the mud that stuck to the boots so that it took a considerable time getting back to our own lines, only to find that the half box of compo rations that had been left for the seven men, had gone missing. The rest of the lads mucked in and shared what they had with us.

That Christmas Day was one to try to forget.

It was only a few days later on an occasion when I was transporting a machine gun to E company, that I encountered this Officer again. The gun and the ammunition had been loaded onto a carrier and at dusk I was making the journey, and met him all alone strolling along the top of the ridge of the hills. He stopped me and said "What have you got there soldier?" And I informed him that I had a machine gun to deliver to E company, whereupon he ordered me to mount the gun on the hill looking out toward the plain and unload the ammunition. He then said "You have a good field of fire there, cover that area." Then tucking his stick under his arm, off he marched leaving me "gob-smacked". I know I have always said that you carry out orders without question, but this had become ridiculous, and as soon as he was out of sight I reloaded everything and continued with my journey.

On my return when I was talking to Ginger and telling him of my experience, he was quite amused and said that only that morning he had also been in conversation with this officer who had told him that he had arranged a football match, between us and the Fusiliers on the German lines to be played on Sunday morning.

It came as no surprise to learn very shortly afterwards that two men in white coats had come and taken him away. The surprise was that this was an officer who had experienced active service before in his career. We were quickly beginning to realise which officers would be able to cope with active service and the few who would not.

Nothing was allowed to move on the plain during the daylight hours, and as the terrain was rather rough the problem of getting rations and equipment to the companies who were right on the edge of the plain fell to the carriers. It was a reasonably pleasant duty so that I volunteered to carry it out on quite a number of occasions together with Pedlar who looked less like a soldier than anyone I know. He had in civilian life being a ladies hairdresser, so that we whiled away the night chatting about our previous occupations with lots of interest on both sides. It is quite a revelation to find out how other sections of people live.

He surprised us all on the occasion when a small battle was ordered to take place to remove the Germans from a farm that was becoming a nuisance to our front line. The bren gun carriers had taken machine guns to give flank fire while a company of men attacked from the front. It was during this operation that they decided to try out a new wireless for communications that could be used with pads on the throat so that the very faintest of whispers, that could not be heard from a few feet away, could be received quite clearly. The leading man of each section of infantry was to carry it but although he could not be heard, it was not difficult to see him with the long ariel pointing skywards, and the first casualties of the action were the three men carrying the wireless sets. This meant that the sections were out of contact with headquarters and a message needed to be got to them quickly that the artillery were to commence bombarding the farm within minutes. Without hesitation Pedlar volunteered to take the message and with bul-

THE IRISH BRIGADE IN TUNISIA.

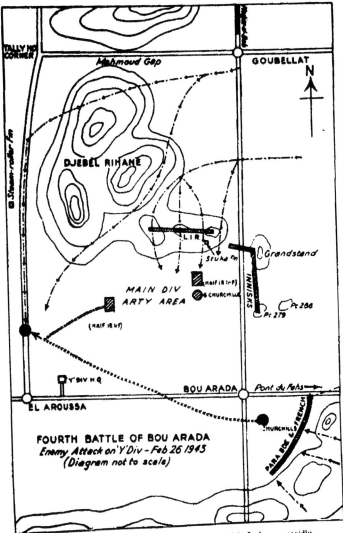

German Tanks from Goubellat having turned our left flank were rapidly advancing on Divisional Headquarters. Churchills racing from "A" arrived at "B," the one point where ambush was possible, just in the nick of time and destroyed six Panzers.

Map of battle area on my day of capture

lets flying all around the place, he casually trotted the two to three hundred yards, when he disappeared into a depression where the men were protected. Then in a couple of minutes was trotting back just as if he was on across-country run. The bravery of this man amazed all his colleagues but it was only the first of many similar incidents. I often wonder why he never got a medal. A brave man without fear.

Our situation remained much the same for the next few weeks until the day of January 20th when it was decided that the Germans should be removed from the position of Two Tree Hill. We had to deliver machine guns very early in the moming to commence the action so that the infantry companies could attack from the front. This was the most awful day of my life. I have never seen such huge casualties and so many deaths. Most of the rest of the day I was ferrying injured men from our medical officer on the field to the brigade first aid station along the road that was under fire, and also attacked by dive bombers, but fortunately I did not come to harm.

The amazing thing to me was the treatment of the men who were brought in with shell shock. The first thing the medical Officer did was to slap them across the face and ask them their name. He continued with this treatment until he got a sensble response from them, explaining that if he could get a responsible answer they were then on the road to recovery. If not? If ever there was an example of being being cruel to be kind this was it.

It was after this action that it was decided that our own officer was not suitable for active service, and he was returned to Algiers to carry out other duties. We were sorry to see him go, but it was probably the best thing for both him and us.

At the end of the day our objective had been achieved, but at great loss of officers and men to our battalion. A battalion of the Grenadier Guards were brought up to relieve us, consolidate the position, and to bury the dead. Our officer was instructed to compile a list of the fatal casualties before they were interned, but he was unable to do this and Fishy volunteered to do the job for him. This was the final reason probably that he was removed from the front lines.

The day after the battle, we were all resting and a group of us were in a deserted Arab building lying on the floor. None of us were sleeping, but not a word was being spoken. We were all probably wishing that the feelings would go away when, unbelievably there was a delivery of mail, most of which had been sent to Scotland and had just caught up with us. Most of the lads had some mail, but Fishy who was lying next to me had only one from his brother asking to meet him in Glasgow on Saturday night. I decided to read out bits of news that I thought could be of interest, only to notice that he had rolled over on his side and was sobbing. It was something of a shock to find that so many brave, good soldiers were shedding tears that day and it was some time before they returned to their normal selves.

In the same post I also received a parcel that had originally contained a fruit pie of gooseberries (that were bottled in the summer because it was well known that this was my favourite fruit). But when it was opened it was probably the original goosberry crumble. I had never seen one before but we all enjoyed it anyway.

Things gradually got back to normal, doing most of the duties that we had got used to before the battle, while the battalion was being brought back into shape by the influx of officers and men from other regiments until the reinforcements from our own regiment could be sent out as replacements. There was the nightly stand to, ration deliveries, equipment deliveries, and the usual visits by Arabs trying to sell eggs or chickens and also trying to scrounge whatever they could from us. One evening a volunteer driver was required to transport an intelligence officer named Ripley who did a feature in a Sunday paper called "Believe it or not". He was going to interview a French schoolteacher at an Arab village well behind the German lines and would have to make his own way back. So, here I go again! At dusk we were off, him with his pencil torch and a map instructing me where to go until till we got within a short distance of the village without any problems. He then climbed down and wished me good luck and goodnight, watching me turn around and disappear from view. Another ship in the night!

I progressed gingerly in what I hoped was the right direction but I was never sure in the dark until I realised that I was slowly going down hill and remaining on a fairly decent track. Then, as I entered a grove of cactus, I saw two very large figures slide out of the shadows in front of me, and stepped sharply on the brakes. After a very short delay that seemed like an age an Irish accent said "Where are you going"? At which, with a great sigh of relief I shouted "Hello Paddy. I'm so relieved to hear your voice"!

They instructed me how to cut across the plain to our lines which were about a couple of miles away, so feeling much better I set off across the plain knowing I was nearly home. Not quite! Some of the tracks were not too good in places, and a steel mesh had been laid to prevent vehicles from sinking in the mud, unfortunately some of the mesh got into the tracks on my carrier and both of them were thrown off. This was rotten luck as it was now impossible to get even one back on, but I set to in the dark and managed to get both of them to the front and laid out ready to be towed back. As it was then starting to get light I covered over with the camouflage netting and decided to wait. I would only move if I was eventually spotted and fired upon.

I suppose it was about an hour later that I saw a motorcycle heading out from our lines across the plain towards me which was unbelievable, somebody obviously was disregarding orders. He soon arrived and it was my pal Ginger who said that he had been keeping a look out for my return when he had spotted the carrier covered over and had borrowed the motorcycle saying "I'm going to fetch him in. Sod the rules!" We sized up the situation and decided that we could probably get the one track on and connected again, so we had a go and it worked. It is amazing what you can do when cornered! In no time at all both tracks were on and I was mobile again, but only just in time as the enemy had now spotted us. As we both roared off with foot down, a few shells started to fall. We both made it, Ginger got a rocket, but it was also almost a pat on the back, and a very large thankyou from me.

We were now in February and there was talk of us being taken out of the line for a rest, and returned to Constantine for a couple of weeks in the very near future. We were looking forward to this with great anticipation, but late one afternoon, Captain Costello and our relief officer, a Captain from the Lancashire Fusiliers came up and said that it was thought that hundreds of Germans were forming up on the hill quite near, ready to make an attack, and that they required one N.C.O. and six men to do a recce and confirm if this was true.

The seven of us were soon ready and on our way, but found no sign of them, and reported back to set up the machine guns, and spray the hill with gunfire to see if there was any response. There was not, so stand-to went on as usual that evening, but we were a little more edgy and very quiet until about four o'clock the next morning, when they attacked with everything they had got and came down that hill like a load of "Banshees" with Schmeisser machine-guns barking out their destruction and all hell breaking loose.

The battle was going on above Fishy and I on a plateau, that we were in a slit trench down the side of, in the gully that the carriers were parked at the other side of in an olive grove. We took no part in the action, that was obviously a short but very fierce encounter that gradually died away, so that we were not quite sure what the situation was. We had been instructed the night before that our paratroops could be helping out with patrols at night and to be aware if we saw them as they did not know the password. So that when the fighting had died down and we saw a patrol, in the camouflage jackets and the helmets that were used by the parras, coming round the bottom of the hill, with great relief we shouted "Come round to your right to miss the mines". We got the reply "Hande augh. Ya Ya Hande augh", We realised that it was too late to do any other with all those guns pointing straight at us. We were then escorted up onto the plateau, where we found that the battle lines had withdrawn about half a mile and were now holding the position they had reached. A group of eight other men had been captured so that we joined them to be told "For you, Tommy, the war is over."

Fishy and I discussed how we could escape and decided to tell their officer in charge that we could get first aid kit and extra blankets for their wounded as there were quite a few of them, if he would allow us to cross the gully to the olive grove where the equipment was. He took quite a lot of persuading especially as there was no common language between us, but eventually he agreed that he would send one of his men with us.

We were sure that we could overcome one guard on the steep track that we had to take and were confident that if we could reach the carriers we could get away. Just when it seemed that it was all systems go, our artillery decided to open up with a heavy bombardment of the German position so that our plot was immediately scuppered.

After spending the night under spasmodic bombardments they decided to evacuate the position and we were lined up in the middle of a section of them to march back to their headquarters. We were made to help the wounded or to carry boxes of ammunition on the trip and, just as we were setting off Fishy and another prisoner were helping ,one on each side of a wounded German when a shell fell near to them killing him but missing them both, so they gently laid him down and everyone carried on. Death on both sides was becoming very cheap!

The officer had collected a haversack full of compo rations that he wanted carrying, so I quickly volunteered thinking that as they all looked alike to us we must look the same to them and it would be difficult for him to remember who had his haversack. I slipped some of the cans to each of us to hide about their person while we were on the move and eventually disposed of it.

It was mid-morning when we arrived at the farm that was their headquarters and we were locked in the barn but had noticed that the most regular Arab visitor selling us eggs was there, quite at home, chatting away to the German officers. When their officer came in looking for his haversack no one responded to his requests so that he looked at each one individually and not finding it, he walked away with a very puzzled look muttering to himself.

Later that day we were all interrogated by an officer who could speak English but as we were only allowed to say our name, rank and number, they got little or no information from us. I was rather surprised when the officer requested to look at my paybook which was in my jacket pocket and, taking out my green hackle he remarked that "This is much better than the one I have so we will swap." There is no point in talking, so that is what happened. Very little importance was attached to feeding us and we were glad the next morning when we were loaded onto a truck and transported into Tunis where there were a few hundred prisoners in a warehouse.

Chapter 11
CAPTIVITY — BEHIND THE WIRE

This was a situation that had not been catered for in the long training that we had, so that I was quite apprehensive about what would happen next. I quickly realised that watches, rings, etc, were to be kept out of sight to prevent them from being confiscated, and that I had to keep a sharp eye out so as not to be at the back of the queue for anything that was going. For example feeding was not a very orderly operation and consisted of one slice of brown bread, one cup of warm brown water called "coffee," in the morning, and approximately 1 pint of a kind of stew with vegetables, mostly onions, and pasta for the main meal.

The local Red Cross came in about every other day with a boiler full of a similar stew and it was again first-come, first-served, but "Devil take the hind most".

The true meaning of the word hunger had taken on an entirely new meaning.

We were supplied with palliases filled with a small amount of straw to use on the concrete floor as a bed. This was purely a reception camp with no facilities for washing and very crude toilets and it was a few days until we were marched down to the docks to board a small Italian cargo boat, with a hold that accommodated about two hundred of us but not with enough room for us to lie down. This was not considered to be a great hardship as the journey to Naples should not take very long.

One tank of water was lowered down for us to drink and we each received one hard biscuit and half a small tin of meat, that was the ration for one day. Early the next morning we set sail out of the harbour, only to race back shortly afterwards as a British convoy was going down the "Med" and so we remained in port for the rest of that day. Three men at a time were allowed to go up the steel ladder to go to the toilet and only when they returned were the next three allowed up, so that in no time at all, the hold was beginning to smell quite awful. On the second day when the queue to the ladder was quite long, "Fishy" turned to me and said "faint!" "Do what?" said I. "Faint " said Fishy, and gathering me up over his shoulder then marched over to the ladder saying "Makeway casualty". The Guard at the top beckoned us up, where I was laid on the deck. Water was requested and granted, then Fishy whispered "take it easy, make it last." The Sun was shining, it was a gorgeous day as we spent about an hour on the deck recovering, before using the toilet then returning to the hold.

The next day Fishy said I'll faint today, but will make it a little later at about feeding time so that if there are any 'buckshees' going we would cop for them. It must have looked an odd sight, because Fishy was a big lad to heave over my shoulder even though I was used to ladder work, but he made sure that his legs were down the ladder side so that he could use them on each rung to help me up. We made it and everything went according to plan, even to getting an extra couple of crusts of bread. It was ten days before the ship could get out of the harbour and cross the Med. to Naples and each day we took it in turns to faint, the amazing thing about this was that no-one else seemed to cotton on to this ruse .This was an early lesson in the art of making life just that little bit more comfortable than it might have been.

The crew of the boat were all Italian and were not very considerate towards prisoners of war, but the men who manned the anti-aircraft guns on the boat were German so that we got on better with them.

When we disembarked in Naples, we were loaded into lorries and taken a short ride to a place called Capua where there was a reception camp for British prisoners of war .

I have often heard the saying "See Naples and die "and I must say the sight of the town with Vesuvious as a background was quite an awesome sight, but I hoped that the second part of the saying was not to come true for a long long time.

The awful sight of the gates closing behind us, the tall wire fencing, the sentry boxes at intervals and at high-level, and the guards, gave me the immediate feeling of a very grim future as it was such a depressing sight . I decided there and then that I would not let the bastards get me down, surely there must be at least a few things to smile about and I would have to get more crafty than I had previously been and retain my sense of humour.

It was an old-established camp, so it was fairly well organised and the prisoners already there were able to instruct us on what was, and what was not permissible. There was of course now another language to try to understand as the Italian guards not only seemed to get very excited when they were giving us orders, but seemed to use their hands as much as their voices to indicate what was needed. This was quite a new experience, but my time in the church choir helped a little as I did understand the odd word or two such as piano when they ordered us to be quiet or presto when they wanted us to hurry. I had quickly learnt my first lesson in yet another language.

We were issued with two blankets each and a straw pallias, then we were allocated beds which were in blocks of six, three decks high on each side of a barrack-type building, with a stove in the centre. This was not in use as the weather was quite good so that we considered the conditions to be pretty luxurious and much better than we had recently suffered. The washing facilities were rather grim — one long steel trough with cold water taps at about 2 ft centres that only trickled very slowly. The toilet block was also quite a surprise, as it was

72

an opening in a concrete floor about six inches wide that went down into an open sewer over which one would squat. We quickly learned that if we needed to use this in the night when it was dark, it was advisable not to be too near to the door, or if you were, to whistle, sing, or have the glow of a cigarette on, as someone always dashed in quickly and without stopping to look, let fly. That was a very simple lesson to learn. There was no work to be done at this camp, so apart from wandering round and round the compound and chatting to each other there was little to occupy our time. It soon became obvious that one or two had got pretty lousy during the last few weeks due to the lack of facilities for keeping clean, so that a lot of the time was spent examining all the seams on the clothes to get rid of the little devils.

We were each given a card to send home with a message on it saying that I was now a prisoner of war and I was OK, which was something of a relief knowing that my family would now be sure what had happened to me. The Red Cross were aware of this camp so that parcels were issued one between two men twice a week. As each parcel was issued the guard pierced every can so that if it was not used pretty quickly it would not be fit to eat and this would prevent prisoners storing food to try to escape. As the food that we were given was very poor and in short supply, the Red Cross parcels were very very welcome. They contained a variety of things depending upon which town they had been sent from, so that we soon knew where to look to find out if we had been lucky enough to get one of the best. Occasionally there was an issue of Canadian Red Cross parcels and these were quite good. In each parcel was a tin of 50 cigarettes which brought great relief to the chaps who were heavy smokers, and cigarettes soon became the biggest currency in the camp.

The gambling instinct in men came out very quickly on parcel days when the chaps with the crown and anchor boards set up their stall to play for cigarettes, and the heavy smokers thought that they could increase their supply by gambling. All around the compound would be little groups until inevitably they would gradually get smaller as the owners of the board got richer. Some of them became tobacco barons and with large supplies of cigarettes could get lots of things not available to the rest of us. Of course the blokes who were desperate for a smoke would be willing to do anything for them to relieve the craving.

I was pretty lucky in this respect as I could smoke when they were available but when they were not, I could still manage quite easily without. It was amazing how terrible this craving must have been to the ones who would turn all their pockets inside out to find a few strands of tobacco that could have fallen out of a dog-end in there, just to roll it up together with the fluff that was also in there and light it to give them a little satisfaction.

There were a number of compounds in the camp some of which were occupied by black Africans who had been captured, and a few of them had a most peculiar pastime of getting through into our compound and walking round looking at each one's shoes then saying "Change your boots, George?" They would offer a small brown bread daily issue and another pair of boots in exchange for ours. This never interested me, but one of the fellows on the next bed changed his boots about five times and eventually finished up with his own again. I have never been able to understand the reasoning behind this exercise.

A lot of these chaps had spent most of their lives in Africa living in their own tribes and tried to carry on with some of their traditions, so that in the evening time it was not unusual to hear them, playing a rhythm on an empty box that sounded something like a drum. The rest of them would be almost stripped off and with braids on their legs and arms made out of parcel string under which they had tied small tins with a few stones in that made a rhythmic noise as they danced. They would go on with these rhythmic dances until they were totally under the spell, so much so in fact that we thought at times that they had access to some kind of a dope. It was quite an experience to see these rituals being carried out. But I'm sure it was something that I would never have seen had I not been in a prison camp.

A number of the prisoners who had been in the camp for some time and were responsible now for quite a bit of the organisation of things, were also reasonable entertainers, and would come into our buildings during the evening together with their accordion and sing a few songs, play tunes, tell a few stories and help to make life a little better.

The weather was quite warm now, we were able to wear very few clothes and were gradually able to get them reasonably clear of livestock. In general we tried our best to get the camp cleaned up and to this end we requested that the blankets should be taken away and fumigated. Eventually this was agreed to so that we were without blankets for about four days until eventually an ox and cart loaded with blankets arrived in the compound and tipped them out into a large heap. When we were instructed to go and get two per person we soon realised that they were now infested with fleas. We can only think that this has been done purposefully to annoy us and they created a very large problem as they are so much more difficult to catch than lice. They got so bad that it was not uncommon to see a chap roll up his bed and take it outside in the middle of the night and throw it away. Every morning we would roll a blanket up tight take it outside and see how many fleas we could catch, but it was impossible to remove all of them. It was not an unusual sight to see the guards put aside their rifle and dive in to catch a flea even when they were on guard duty, but they seemed much more able to live with this situation than we were, probably because they had always been used to them.

They were quite a peculiar looking lot these guards, I suppose they were the worst of the Italian army that were not suitable for active service, but they could be most cruel on occasions when someone had made an unsuccessful attempt to escape. Some of the lads were affected pretty badly by becoming prisoners and made attempts to escape that would be impossible, such as trying to climb over the wire and such like, but it was not unusual when they were caught for them to be fastened to a post by the main gate and left in the hot sunlight all day without access to a drink. They could be quite cruel sods! It was queer to see them lining up on parade prior to coming on duty as they seemed to be a mixture of very tall or very short men, some wearing breeches and putties and some wearing a type of plus four trousers and putties — very very untidily dressed and often unshaven, invariably the very tall men had a rifle about three feet long and had to bend to hold it, while the very short men had a rifle about 5 ft long and had to reach up to hold it, so that on parade they were quite an amusing sight.

We were counted every morning and every evening and two guards were left to walk around in the compounds each evening. It was this exercise that prompted two chaps to attempt an escape that was unexpectedly successful. They had acquired enough Italian uniforms to get by in a poor light and had made the equipment from the cardboard of the Red Cross parcels, and a rifle that was shaped from one of the bedboards. As the guards were changed in each compound two men fell out to stay, and the other two fell in to be marched out of the gate, so that as they approached the main gate these two prisoners fell in at the rear and marched out without it being noticed that they had two extra men. They got away from the camp and were away for 48 hours, but unfortunately they were then caught and brought back to be punished on the stake by the gate. There were a number of ingenious attempts but none of them were successful unfortunately. The best one was one that I was told about that had happened before we arrived. Someone had found that there was a sewer manhole cover that was not fastened down in a compound that led down to quite a large sewer that could be negotiated, and they had arranged for a disturbance to be carried out at the other end of the compound one evening so that they could go down it and away. But everything did not quite go according to plan, for once they were down, there was a little queue of chaps with their kit waiting to descend into the manhole. Of course they were spotted and the alarm raised, so that the few that did get away and try to raise manhole covers to get out when they were beyond boundaries of the camp, were surprised to find troops waiting for them. It was a great idea but such a pity that it had not succeeded.

Although building was going on all the time at the camp, I was very interested to see how they did this work, as the walls were constructed of the ash from the volcano that was quarried and cut into blocks all regular size. It was used to build in a similar manner to the breeze blocks that were used in England. This was then plastered over which was a job that these people were very expert at.

The camp was beginning to look rather crowded and it was decided that we should be sent to another camp that was about half-way up country over to the Adriatic side, and we were dispatched by train to Campo Conccentramento P.G. 53 at Macerata.

Chapter 12
MAKING THE BEST OF IT

We packed our bit of kit and were herded into the wagons in the railway siding for the journey. Once again it was not considered necessary to provide food for the journey, but we had become experienced by now so that there was always a little reserve of food tucked away in case of emergencies. The heat in the packed trucks was pretty grim and we were glad when we pulled into the siding next to the camp, where we were unloaded and shepherded into a huge camp of between seven and eight thousand men.

It was great to quickly realise that it was a well-established camp that consisted of quite a number of large warehouse-type buildings, in a very large area of ground that was even big enough to accommodate a football pitch. The blocks of six beds were arranged into groups identified by numbers for the purpose of being counted, fed, and the issue of parcels or post that was supervised by our own N.C.O.s. This was quite a good arrangement that made life so much better organised.

They were pretty high buildings so that I was lucky to be on the top deck with a fellow called Braun. Fishy and I had been parted during the move, two Scottish lads were on the middle deck, one named Billy Black, who had been the centre forward for Dundee United, and two Manchester lads on the bottom deck. They were an amusing couple as the one considered himself a tattoo artist and the other one, who was not very bright, being his model. He would draw a design, then with three needles in a cork, and a bottle of blue ink, he would tattoo his design onto his mate called Smoking Joe, telling him that he would have to add the different colours after the war. It was getting quite hard to find a space on him to put a new design but he did not seem to mind and never complained.

The two Scotsman used to swap one bread ration each day for cigarettes and share their other one as they were both really addicted to the 'weed' and could stand the hunger rather than having no smokes.

There was a variety of talent in the camp that provided concert parties of brilliant turns. If you closed your eyes during them you could hear the voices of Vera Lynn, Gracie Fields, Bing Crosby, Paul Robeson, Jack Buchanan, Arthur Askey, or Tommy Trinder. Some of the female impersonators were fantastic with the blonde wigs made out of parcel string and the dresses that I still have no idea what they were made from. They certainly put on some very good shows that were also enjoyed by the Italian officers at the camp.

I made a friend of one of the comedians, whose name really was Jack Frost. He did monologues in the style of Jack Warner who had at that time the catch phrase of 'mind my bike,' so that when Frosty got a large boil on his chest, we drew a white and blue ring around the bright red centre and wrote underneath across his stomach 'Mind My Boil' in large letters. That is how he went on the stage carrying a large suitcase out of which he took a dog-end, lit it and started to perform the stuff that I had written for him. That went something like this:

This is the tale of camp 53
A host of forgotten men
Where a careful Yid went a solo
On an Ace, King, Queen, Jack, Ten.

Billet s were so overcrowded
Mice had to run round the walls,

and Bugs as big as Grant tanks
played hopscotch round you're balls.

It is a camp of great despair
A camp of hopeless hope
Where many a young lad had his ring snatched
through dropping his bar of soap.

This went on for about twenty or so verses, getting him a reasonable applause and managed to raise a few smiles. I lost connection with Jack in the melee later on, and another ship had passed.

The routine of this camp was much the same as before and the food that they supplied was about the same. If it had not been for the Red Cross parcels we should have gradually starved, as it was, everyone had that permanent hungry feeling.

A lot of fellows fell victims to dysentery which reduced them to almost skeletons, and they used to attend the medical centre that was staffed by our men. As it only had limited supplies of equipment they could only be given extra milk and arrowroot to try to build up their strength. One day a decent artist did a full sized graffiti drawing of the film star William Powell on the wall at the other side of the door where these men queued up and had written at the side 'They call him the Thin Man'. The film had been recently made and it was quite an amusing live caricature.

There must have been some sort of radio in the camp somewhere and a sergeant used to come around most evenings to give out the news of the war which was at last getting better in the Middle East. The first time I heard his very familiar accent I soon found out that he lived only a few miles from me and he was able to tell me where to find another local fellow who was the barber in another block. The next day I found him and was so surprised to find that we had previously worked together. He was a stonemason who had carved some inscriptions on the stones in a church that we had built.

Being a worker he got extra rations of the daily soup and sometimes he saved a pot of it for me, which was great, every little extra was very welcome.

The most popular pastime in the camp was tin-bashing, which went on constantly all day except for the two hours in the middle of the day, which was siesta time for the Ities, and strict silence was the order of the day for these two hours.

It was amazing what could be made from empty tins using only stones or bits of wood as hammers and, occasionally a pair of nail scissors that had to be concealed, and of course, the little tin opener. The masterpiece was the Klim Clock that was fixed on the concrete pillar next to my bed. It kept perfect time and had tins of water suspended on string as weights and the pendulum was balanced on the edge of a razor blade. It was not unusual to see the Italian officers checking their watches by it. Another useful invention was the blower which was like a miniature blacksmith's hearth, operated by a small fan made in a tin with blades inside and gears turned with string and a handle made out of bent wire. They were great with wood - embers stolen from the cookhouse fire which could be used like charcoal to boil water, to heat the tins, or to make tea, without making any smoke or noise, so that they were our sort of secret weapon.

Everyone had a drinking mug made out of a tin, but with a lid and handle, and some of them were quite elaborate. Everything that could be made from tins was made, even to small suitcases, so that the noise for most of the day was worse than being in a busy factory. The ingenuity of some of the fellows never ceased to amaze me — some of the art work was quite spectacular and the tin replica of the F A cup was something special. Occasionally we had a programme of boxing, and there were a few that had been budding professionals before they had been captured. I remember one pretty well — Darky Hughes who was in the class of Boon and Danahar whose careers had been cut short by the outbreak of war. The bouts were only three rounds long as the fitness of the men could only manage this, and the prize for the winner was a few fags and an extra bread ration. The shows were a very welcome diversion from the day by day monotony.

Chapter 13
To Hell And Back

Things got very exciting early in September, when we learned that Italy had been invaded, and in no time at all they had capitulated.

We were very elated. The guards disappeared, the gates were open, and rumours were flying around regarding the repatriation. Eventually the senior officers in the camp got the tannoy working and gave the instructions to stay put, and that an orderly evacuation would be arranged by the British troops as soon as this was possible. "Keep off the roads, and avoid causing chaos to the occupying army". We did wander out to get the feeling of freedom and to pick grapes from the vinyards close by. Although quite a number of fellows decided to get away, the majority stayed in the camp to await the arrival of our troops. When we found a store of sheets, they were issued to the rest of us and the Red Cross parcels were shared around. We took our beds outside and slept under the stars with a great feeling of anticipation. Free at last! Home soon!

This feeling was shattered at about two o'clock in the morning — all hell broke loose as a large convoy of German armoured cars, and troops in lorries arrived with machine guns blasting. The gates were locked and the sentry boxes were manned with troops armed with large machine guns. It is difficult to describe the feeling of disappointment, and there were actually a few suicides before morning. We soon learned that although the Italians had packed it in, the Germans were going to continue to defend the whole of Italy. There are no words to describe the feelings of depression that were all over the camp.

Within a few days we were all loaded onto a long train of cattle trucks, with 42 men per truck, to be transported to Germany. This was to be a long, long, slow journey as the railway lines were crowded with troops and material travelling south, and trains of prisoners travelling north. The only thing that put a bit of a smile on anyone's face was when we were parked in a siding that was full of similar trains, we saw that some of them were filled with Italians who were now prisoners themselves.

The very short, total elation of being free, was so cruelly dashed. Being locked in a cattle truck with only bread and water and no facilities at all, for a journey to goodness knows where, or for how long, induced the lowest feeling that I could remember especially as I could not think of any way at all that some small advantage could be made in this situation. The future looked very black and even more so as we were travelling north towards the Alps which we were going to have to cross, and there were already white caps upon these mountains. With the arrival of the cold weather the depression was getting worse. As there were no sanitary facilities in the trucks, and very few holes for ventilation. These were covered with barbed wire, the door was only opened to pass in water and bread and the atmosphere was getting indescribable .We were desperately trying to remove the boards from the floor of the truck but they were very strong and presented a difficult problem due to our lack of tools. We did eventually manage to get a hole through that was just about large enough to dispose of our of obnoxious rubbish, so that at last this was our first little improvement.

It was almost a week's tortuous travelling from the reasonable warmth of Italy to the awful large reception camp number 7A, at a place called Moosberg not far from Munich. This was a large depressing old-established camp, and was our first introduction to guards walking around with guard dogs on leads that were Alsatians and Doberman Pinchers. They were well trained to be very vicious animals that needed to be avoided. It seemed to give the guards great pleasure to loose them into the huts first thing in the morning when they had called us out for counting, so that they could see the lads diving out through windows,doors, or the nearest opening — with trousers off, or in the process of getting dressed. I must confess that it presented a bloody awful picture. They were pretty efficient at organisation at this camp and we were all registered and given a prisoner of war number. Mine being 154100. We were all medically examined and even given an innocculation in the chest which was something of a surprise, but a bigger surprise was the fact that a clean needle was used for each man. The food was no improvement but was different, the slice of bread was much darker in colour and a very peculiar flavour, and the stew was pretty grim. Cabbages, a few spuds — just as they had come from the ground, and dried swedes. These had obviously been for animal feed and looked like little strips of leather lace that swell up considerably when boiled, and tasted bloody awful. Once a week it was supposed to contain meat, but if you were lucky enough to find some it was cause for celebration. The only favourable thing that can be said is, it was rather filling.

We were sent to a stone quarry for two days running, to break rocks and load them into trucks, where we gave a very good imitation of a film on the slowest of slow motions so that this work did not continue and we were soon dispatched to a camp at the far eastern side of Austria. It was out in the wilds and miles from anywhere and had only been occupied by the Russians previous to our arrival and was not known to the Red Cross. It was a terrible camp and the weather was now getting very cold. Three hundred men were allocated one bed in a room that had been a stable for 12 horses. There were three decks with 50 men to each side and there were only six

One big bed, and 300 men

small windows, none of which would open, and one door. Needless to say the air in the place, especially first thing in the morning, was a bit thick. I was fortunate enough to get a place on the top deck as there was a little more room between that and the ceiling than there was on the lower two decks.

One of the first operations after we arrived was to visit the showers. They took all our clothes away for fumigation, then we were done over by Russian prisoners with very fine hair clippers from the tip of our toes to the top of our heads until there was not a hair anywhere to be seen — only a few little nicks from negotiating awkward parts. Following this, and looking like beings from outer space, we went through a door way to the showers where there was a fellow each side of the door with a bucket of disinfectant and a washing-up mop, with which he doused us under the crutch and under the arms, so that you can imagine the cries of anguish that this caused. Just as the pain was easing off we stepped under the hot shower which brought it all back again. Bloody hell! What next! We had to wait some time for our clothes, in a building of arched brick walls and roof with no windows and a steel door, but it was quite an amusing sight. A room full of nude men in leather boots and belts with not a hair in sight, and the odd lumps and bumps never seen before .The big lads were walking about with their hands behind their backs while the little fellows seemed to be more bashful. Where on earth the playing cards came from I shall never know but there were soon small groups of lads squatting and playing cards, so that it was easy to see which one was the dealer even from the rear by what was swinging underneath. It was really a very grim experience, but we managed to get a bit of a laugh by checking to see if what they say about the fellows with the biggest feet was really true. Not always! But some of those shoes must have pinched those big chaps.

The Russians in the camp got no recognition by their country and were really starving to death. An ox cart was used to collect the rubbish every day and it came down the track between the compounds which led down to the field outside the camp, and the rubbish was dumped into a large trench that had been dug there. It was a shock to see that when it stopped at the gate to the Russian compound, they came out with a naked dead body and threw it into the rubbish cart. That was the way that they buried their dead, at least one a day but often more that. They had probably carried this man on parade between two others for some days after he died so that he would be counted for the meagre rations that they got, and only when it was impossible to do this any longer would his body be thrown away. Their treatment was pretty awful and on one occasion when two dogs were moved into their compound for the night as was the usual practice, two dogs skins were found on the barbed wire the next morning, and I can only guess what became of the rest of their bodies.

Winter was well on its way by now and Christmas must have come and gone, or have been cancelled as I have no recollection of it, but hopefully spring was around the corner. I really was beginning to think that my luck had run out and when I got really depressed I had only to compare my lot with that of the Russians to realise that I was far luckier than them. It had been like one long depressing dark night since September and not fit for any ships to be out.

This camp was most depressing, but as working parties were being dispatched regularly from here I hoped that pretty soon my number would be on the list. One day there was a list of about 50 which included all the chaps that I knew but stopped at the number before mine and they left to go to work in the coal mines in Silesia. Now I was pretty anxious to see the next list which came up a couple of days later for 14 men, and I was the first on the list with 13 strangers. Nothing could be worse than this camp so that I was really glad to be leaving it behind, whatever the future held.

We were a very scruffy half-starved looking crew that left the camp with three guards and their dogs to eventually board an ordinary train. It was strange lined up on a platform with civilians going about their daily business, trying to ignore us, and was so different to see men, women and children behaving normally again. There is a world outside!

Chapter 14

LIFE IN AUSTRIA

We eventually arrived in Vienna at about six o'clock in the morning and had to change stations, which meant a walk across the city. We were very surprised to see how many people were around at that time in the morning. I'm afraid the beauty of the place did not impress us as much as it should have, and we must have looked a queer group with a tin chattels hanging from our rucksacks, as we were herded along the street. We were given a drink of what they called coffee and some bread and soft cheese, then we boarded another train that stopped at every station along the way. Eventually we arrived at a station in a very beautiful area of the country at the side of a very large lake, where we disembarked and boarded a ferry to cross the lake to St. Wolfgang which was almost our destination.

We were to be felling trees in forests a few miles up in the mountains and we were taken to the office of the estate owner who we were to work for, which was next to the church in the small town. He interviewed us and took the particulars — names, addresses, what work we had done before, and was very surprised to find that there were Englishmen who had to work for a living, as the only ones that they were acquainted with were the Prince of Wales and his friends who used to holiday there. They thought that all Englishmen were similar, and wore top hat and tails. He told us that he had requested 14

The fourteen lucky guys who landed in Sswarzensee. Johann, centre front; Lenny, Corporal, Ray, Dickie, Burnikel, Johnno, the author, Brummie Sam, Huttie, Sergeant Dickson, Johann Lee, Ted and Dudley

men for work as the previous ones had gone sick or were no longer able to work, and when he was informed that there were only British prisoners available he had agreed to take us on the understanding that if we could not do the work he would return us to the camp. He did not realise what an incentive this was for us to try. We quickly realised that their opinion of the British could probably be used to our advantage if we were crafty enough, and when I was asked what my job had been I had said I was a decorator, thinking that builders could possibly be required in the bomb damaged cities.

After the preliminaries had been finished we were introduced to the two soldiers who were to guard us, and Johann the civilian lumberjack who was to be our work boss. We then began the journey to our billet which was begun at a very gentle stroll as we were by now pretty knackered and unfit. The road rose slowly from the town eventually leaving the dwellings behind and going on to a small track. We had to rest about every 20 minutes and after passing some farm buildings we got on to a steep rocky track up the side of the mountain. There were small shrines where the guards did their little rituals and we just rested. Eventually we came to a smaller but still a large lake called Schwarzensee where there was a small wooden house and a guest house which was closed for the war but only opened in the summer. We carried on round the lake to the other end at the foot of the mountains, and about 300 yards up a grassy valley was the typical Austrian mountain lodge that was to be our base. As we were all totally shattered after the journey, this looked like heaven and I had the strange feeling that Lady Luck was rousing from a deep sleep.

Two of the rooms in the billet had raised platforms along

Johnno, Pickie, Sam, Ray, Brummie Ted and the author on the day of the deer shoot

Loading the logs and clearing the snow off with the shovels we were to ride on

one side that had to serve as beds. The one downstairs for nine men had a large tiled cooking range in it, and the small one upstairs for five, had a small stove. Another large room downstairs was for the guards and Johann and there was also a small cellar which was to be very useful later on.

The washing facility was a large tree trunk hollowed out as a trough which was fed by constant running water that came down wooden pipes from the stream higher up the mountain. It led to a wooden stand pipe with a spout that discharged into the trough at one end and overflowed at the other forming a small stream to flow back into a larger stream down the valley to the lake. The toilet was in the small hut fixed onto two small tree trunks across the stream and with a wooden footbridge to it. This indeed was luxury — a bog with running water and baths as often as we wish, albeit very cold, but great. It looks as if Christmas might only have been postponed.

Johann and family on a Sunday morning climb to the top of Schaffberg with Ted, Ray and Sam

We soon settled in and appointed the oldest member, Nutty, to be cook and billet orderly, to generally look after the place, and it was agreed that he would not be expected to do any other work. Johann introduced us to our tools, axes sharp enough to shave with, large cross cut saws that he also kept very sharp, and a tool for turning and moving logs, that was like a large steel eagles beak on the end of a beech handle. So off we set on the next morning after washing, shaving, and having breakfast, up into the woods where we were to clear an area. We were shown how to fell a tree to the exact position that you wanted it to fall.

As we were not too far away we were able to return at lunch time for tea and whatever else there was, then back to work in the afternoon until about 5.30 when we washed, got fed, then rested playing bridge or card games or any other way of passing the time before going to bed. It was getting chilly in the evenings but we now had an unlimited supply of firewood so that we were really comfortable.

All the windows were barred as was the usual in this area of

On the summit of 'Heaven's Gateway'

Austria and the rear door was steel and was locked at about 8 o'clock every evening, so that if we required to go to the toilet after then we had to go out through the guards room and the front door.

In a few days came the first Saturday morning and as usual the guards called us to get outside ready for work, but we said, "What is going on? This is Saturday and Englishman do not work on Saturdays." They went into a short discussion and decided that as we also had to collect the rations from St. Wolfgang, as long as there were four men to go to the town with the guard, that this would be the only usual Saturday duty. The rest of the lads could be doing their washing and cleaning up. This had certainly to be a first as I could not remember anyone before having a five day working week.

Naturally I was one of the volunteers to go to the town to collect the rations and the guard had charge of our ration cards. The reason for this was that a party of less than 20 prisoners was not supplied with their food from the company but were given ration cards to collect it from the local shops. There was also a system of rationing in Austria where the people who did the heaviest work got the most rations on a sliding scale down to housewives who got the least. Miners and timber workers were in the heaviest working class so that we got heaviest worker rations.

It was a much easier journey down to town where we were to collect these large round loaves of rye bread, butter, fat, vegetables, and the meat which I wanted to carry. This turned out to be a kilo per man, so that when I went into the shop with the guard to collect it, the butcher beckoned us to go through to the rear of the shop where he packed my rucksack with veal so that his customers would not see how much meat we got. That was to be my load to carry back. 14 kilos was quite enough to manage on this first trip. We then called in the post office to see if there was any mail for the guards. We had to wait down in the outbuildings below the estate office while the guard reported to them and got his orders for the week.

Nosing around I found that there was a large store of potatoes at the other side of the timber wall, about 8 ft high, that belonged to the military who had a number of hospitals and convalescent homes for wounded and sick personal in the hotels in the town. We immediately decided that it would eventually need five men at least to fetch the rations instead of four in the future and we were only able to steal a few spuds on this trip. It was a long, hard trip back, with lots of rests on the way but we had unlimited time and we were certainly not going to complain. We soon got into this way of life and were getting stronger every day. We learned a lot about trees, how they grew, what each type was, and the best way to fell them, so that it was becoming enjoyable work the more we got used to it.

We would fell the trees, then remove all the branches, cut them into six metre lengths, and remove the bark which had to be done very carefully so that they could be rolled and stacked to be taken away to make artificial leather. We would then make large stacks of the logs to stay there until the winter

Work finished and time to relax

Our billet in Austria, looking very tidy and unchanged after fifty years

Our washing and bathing facility, still working after fifty years

The cellar window that was so useful can just be seen above ground level

when the local farmers could come with their oxen and sleighs to cart them down to the timberyard. The beech trees were to be cut into four and a half metre lengths to be used for railway sleepers, and all the timber that was left after these operations would be cut into one metre lengths and stacked for fuel. I think it was something of a surprise to find that we could manage this type of work, but we soon were able to do it pretty well. In fact we got so good at it that we were allowed to take a motor saw, when petrol was available, to cut the firewood. Somehow, unfortunately, we always got the railway sleeper timber mixed up with the firewood timber and could not understand why we always had a short half metre left. We never did manage to quite understand the system and no railway sleeper timber was ever produced.

This was quite a heathy life, and with the supply of Red Cross parcels beginning to arrive at the Post Office, we began to live fairly well. Par-boiled potatoes, then fried, with veal, spam or bully beef, was the most popular meal, but we could not steal quite enough spuds to have these every day. Nutty eventually became quite a reasonable cook and we managed very well.

We found out that some of the farmers managed to get white flour and we could exchange cigarettes for this, but we were very limited in how we could use this without baking powder. However we found that the only treatment that we could get for stomach problems was bi-carbonate of soda which would do the job nicely, so I went sick. I was taken down to the medical officer in town and it worked wonderfully well. He gave me a large box of the stuff so that we were able to cook a few treats occasionally. The evening's were never a problem as we had board games and cards to pass away the time and had a small amount of paraffin to light the late evenings, and we became very good at finding our own amusement. Johann had his zither that he used to play in the evenings and produce the most lovely Austrian music to which he would sing the local songs for us. This was a good

*Jonno, Sam and Ted outside the house of Johann, with his wife and son, Joseph.
Note the pair of home-made skis propped against the wall*

way of spending an evening and also helping to understand the language. As a matter of fact I quickly learned how to sing a couple of the songs, even though I did not understand most of the words.

It is the custom in Austria for the farmers to send their cattle up into the mountains for the whole of the summer with one young lady to look after them. In the late spring three lots of them arrived in the cow huts in the next valley.

The more adventurous of us decided at this time that a walk in the evening was a good idea and we eventually found ourselves round in the next valley offering to help in any way we could in the very heavy work that these young ladies used to carry out. They had to cut down bracken for the bedding, milk the cows morning and evening, then make butter and cheese from the milk that they gave. Once a week the farmer would come up with his load on his back to bring supplies, then to take down to the farm the butter and cheese that had been produced. We soon realised that there was both butter and buttermilk to be had by doing a few jobs to help. Not only this, we

The landing stage at the White Horse Inn, St. Wolfgang

The ferry boat arriving at the White Horse Inn landing stage at St. Wolfgang

also had the company of young ladies, very reluctant at first but probably time will alter that we hoped.

We had not been here very long before they decided that the two guards were young enough to join the forces on their eastern front where they were having a rather rough time, so it was two rather depressed fellows that left and two older ones took their place. Both of them came from Austria and soon realised that they had found a very good job. They were also more relaxed about things, so that we were able to have a little more freedom than we had had previously, and it was only when they knew that an inspection was to be made by their officers that they saw to it that everything was in order. We even managed to do a bit of fishing in the lake that was stocked with roach and perch and had quite a few large pike in it too. Only very special people were allowed to fish in the lake but there was no-one to deter us, providing we took care. There was one occasion when a high ranking German officer had been given permission, and without warning as we were at one end of the lake one Sunday morning, his boat came

The lake where we worked, swam and fished. The small house and the hotel can be seen at the top right

round and he saw us. We quickly made off to the billet but he had found our home-made rods and brought them up to the camp when we denied any knowledge of them. He had said that he was going to report the matter and that the guards would probably be punished. When the estate boss heard about this he said "I will attend to it and the officer will never get permission to come fishing here again." We are now beginning to realise that we are very much in favour with our boss.

It was shortly after this that I really did have to report sick with my leg. It appeared that the same complaint that I had in my wrist some time ago was now affecting my leg. So with the help of a stick, I made my way with a guard to the doctor in the town to examine it. He decided to put it in a splint which he made of a sort of wire frame that he fastened on with the paper bandages that they had to use. They were a sort of crepe paper and were quite strong. He bound me up with these bandages then said "OK keep that on till it is better". The guard informed him that we now had about four miles to walk up the mountains back to the camp, at which he commenced to remove the bandages and made them up into a small parcel. He then gave me the metal splint and a jar of the black stuff that he had applied to my leg and told me to put them back on when I got back to camp and rest until it was better.

I complained to the guards that it was because of the wooden clogs that we had to wear to work, that were most difficult on the mountain sides, that had caused the problems with my leg and the boss immediately agreed that we should all be supplied with mountain boots. Seven men were to attend to the shoemakers shop on the following Saturday morning. And seven men on the following Saturday morning, even Nutty the cook got mountain boots, so now we were much better off whenever we were out walking. Even Johann was jealous of the boots that we wore as his were getting a little worse for wear. Ted, one of the lads, had been a cobbler himself before he had been called up into the army and he agreed that if he could get the material he would strip down a pair of his boots and rebuild them for him. It was pretty amazing to see him work, even making the waxed threads himself. Some new soles were found from somewhere and eventually Johann had boots just as good as ours.

I was amazed at the speed that my leg got well again and very soon I was back in circulation since then I have always wondered what the black stuff was. It certainly worked for me.

In the next valley was a stone quarry that was being worked by three Italian workers and produced the most beautiful red, black, white and brown marble, that was used in most of the buildings in the locality for a variety of things such as window sills and kitchen surfaces. They had asked our boss if one of the prisoners was capable of building a stone building that could be locked up and would contain the tools and explosives so that they would be more secure. When the request was put to us I agreed to carry out this work, so that for the next few weeks I left every morning to go round to the next valley, and had three Italian labourers working for me, cuffing the stones that I needed, and we built the shell of their new store in marble stone. This was the first time that I had built a marble hall. They had some different foods to us and I enjoyed lunch with them every day that I worked there. They were also very good at tickling trout in the stream down the valley, and on occasions we had fish for lunch, not bad. This was quality ,a pleasant interlude, but I was soon back into the swing of things in the camp.

It was about this time that the people in town had started speaking to us secretly and they all were requesting to know when the second front would be starting on the continent. For some unknown reason, one of the Geordies had always said that this would be the sixth of June.

Johann had been home for the night on the day before, so that very early on the 6th when we heard a yodel from a long way away and eventually saw him at the bottom of the track with his stick in the air and virtually trotting up towards us. We wondered what on earth was going on until he got near enough to shout and say "they've started and landed in France. Yippie!" The difference in the attitude of the local people towards us after this was quite noticeable and I am sure they thought that we had a direct line to England. We did not enlighten them by telling them that this had been a pure guess.

Parcels were arriving from home and eventually I got one myself. Although the folks at home were allowed to send a parcel every three months and this was done, I only ever got one and it did contain the only thing that I had ever requested, along with the woolly socks, ballaclavas, and warm clothes, my suit of pyjamas that would make sleeping in those rough blankets so much better. The other lads all seemed to be getting cigarette parcels, but although my family had a regular order with the tobacconist to send two hundred cigarettes per month, I only received one parcel of two hundred and that was from the regiment. Cigarette parcels were so easily recognised but I often wonder if all of them were dispatched. Some of the fellows always said that the ones that arrived were

A view of the area showing the mountains surrounding St. Wolfgang. Strobe can be seen at the far end of the oake where King Leopold was released

packed at home and sent without identification marks and that this was the reason that they arrived safely. This did not concern me too much as I could do without, but they were always useful as currency — far better than money.

We had been warned by Johann about the fellow who lived at the other end of the lake with his wife and family of small children and looked after the control of the water flowing from the lake and down pipes to the small hydro-electric power station in the valley. He had been injured by the loss of his hand in a timberyard so that he was unfit for military service. He had always been a very loyal party member and he was not to be trusted. He always wore a large revolver on his belt and if a guard was to be away in the evening he would come to the camp to act as a relief guard. We quickly realised that he was a very heavy smoker and that this could influence the way that he treated us.

One Monday morning Johann came back from his weekend at home with the instructions that we had to fell trees at the far side of the lake with which we were to construct a log cabin for one of the boss's female friends. This was to be in a small wooded area on the opposite side of the lake. Off we went to sort out the correct type of very tall slim trees that would be ideal for this purpose, soon we had enough ready to slide down to the waters edge where we were to float them across behind the flat bottom boat to the other side of the lake.

It was quite a difficult job to chain them together without going into water, but as it was quite warm we did not mind and quickly stripped off down to the buff and enjoyed swimming around getting them all together. We spent quite a pleasent day towing them across the lake and stacking them ready for building to start. We had imagined that as there was no-one about, that our nude swimming had not been seen, but when we spoke to the cow girls later on they quickly made it known that they had been amused the sight of us in the nude.

The construction of the log cabin became a spare time job only to be carried out when there were not more important jobs to be done, but it came along very well and was quite an experience to see how they built their log cabins and in no time at all it was up to eave level. We were also shown how to make wooden shingles for the roof and how to select the proper trees for this purpose, so that Sam became quite an expert at this job and enjoyed spending some of his spare time getting enough made for the roof.

One of our guards got sick about this time and had to go into hospital. So once again we had the problem of getting a new guard into our way of living, but as this one was also a heavy smoker, the problem was not too difficult. Shortly after his arrival, he got a letter back that he had written to his son who was serving on the Russian front that had not been delivered. On the back of it, in pencil it said "died fighting for the Fatherland". This was the only information that he recieved to say that his son had been killed in action. He was quite disgusted by this and then went out of his way to make things more comfortable for us.

One weekend, the boss and a few of his friends arrived with three girls. They sent the guards and Johann all home until Monday morning so that they would have somewhere to sleep, and quite a lively weekend took place at the camp. It made it quite understandable that a log cabin would be an ideal gift for a girl friend so that they could spend weekends together. There was very little sleeping done of course, by our visitors or ourselves, and I wondered if there was not something in the Red Cross regulations that prevented them from inflicting such a torture on very fit young men who were starving, but not for food.

Shortly after this, a shoot was to take place and a few high-ranking officers came up with a few friends of the boss for a day's shooting at which we were to be used as beaters. We had to spread out in the woods and drive any deer that were in there down towards the specially constructed shooting lodges where they were waiting. We did manage to get a few deer down but only one was shot on the day, and then we all returned to the camp and had a few drinks as payment for our services. They were only interested in the antlers and the skull of the deer to mount upon the wall, the remainder had to be taken down to the meat control in the town on the next day. As a volunteer was required for this purpose, I decided that it could be a good way of spending a day different to the norm.

The next morning I met the gamekeeper on the site where he loaded the deer in a harness onto my back and instructed me to call at his house on the way down and drop off the heart and liver for his wife. It was a lovely day and although the load was pretty heavy it was not too bad going down, and I was now getting very fit. I only met one fellow before I got to the outskirts of the town and he was only interested in the long hair down the centre of the back that they used to make the brush with which they decorated their hats. My pay from the gamekeeper for this job was one of these brushes. I had a very good day and was able to try to converse with the natives which helped quite a lot.

St. Wolfgang im Salzkammergut

Im „Wei - ßen Rös - sl" am Wolf - gang -
see, dort steht das Glück vor der Tür

108

The farmers now realised that they could get some cheap labour if they asked for prisoners to help them, and the farmer that had the farm on the track down to the town requested six prisoners for a couple of days to help him. We arrived early in the morning and were given various tasks about the farm mostly clearing up and a little maintenance that had been neglected for some time. It was a change and a surprise to find that the morning had gone by so quickly when we were called in for lunch. We were to eat with them in the huge kitchen that had a very large scrubbed table towards the corner of the room with benches along the side. On the wall in this corner was a small crucifix that they used to pray to when they had their meals. When we were all in there, ready for lunch, the farmer, his wife, and a couple of workers stood there for what seemed like ages to us, reciting the words that were said before meals. When this was finished, the farmer's wife brought in a very large bowl of soup. Everyone round the table had a large spoon and fed themselves straight from the bowl. This was alright for the locals, they were quite used to it and never spilled a drop. In fact it seemed to noisily jump the last few inches from the spoon to their mouths, but we were not so expert so therefore we were a little bit unfortunate that the bowl was empty long before we had managed to get a fair share. This completed, she then set a piece of wood on the centre of the table on which she placed the largest frying pan that I have ever seen. It was full of fried potatoes and small pieces of bacon. Once again they proceeded with the same spoon to serve themselves from the frying pan and were uncannily clever at balancing quite a number of pieces on one spoon while we were juggling with one piece, trying carefully to prevent it from falling off before it got to our mouths. This was quite a new experience in the way that they behaved, and Johann had a quiet word with the farmer's wife afterwards to

A good view of St. Wolfgang and the church. The words of the song are very appropriate to my story

tell her that we always ate with knives and forks off a separate plate each.

It was a surprise the next day when we were called in to lunch to find that she had taken to heart what he had said and that there were two tables in the kitchen, one for them and one for us, but the procedure was just the same. We had just one bowl for the soup and one smaller frying pan for the potatoes and bacon, but we gave her full marks for trying and we did manage a little more food each, which was a good feeling. Life went along comfortably during the rest of the summer and the news that we were hearing was very good so that we were beginning to look forward to the end of the war and getting back to England.

It was at about that this time that the powers that be, decided that our spiritual needs wanted some attention and that a prisoner of war padre should visit us for a day, to this end. He arrived early one evening with one guard and was to spend the night in the guesthouse at the other end of lake that the owner, the butchers wife, was spending a bit of time cleanimg and airing. That evening was spent talking and we arranged that there would be no work the next day, but that it would be devoted to spending time with the padre.

He came up early the next morning and we showed him all around, and surprised him with the good facilities that we enjoyed, especially when it came to lunch time and we were able to put on a very decent meal. The day went fairly quickly and he expressed his delight at the way he had been treated and expressed his surprise at the conditions that existed for us. We decided to give him a bigger surprise by asking him if he would prefer to go swimming or fishing, or possibly both. He decided that a swim would be great and quite a change, so that we managed by using a balaclava, with a little modification, as a costume for him, and went down for a swim in the lake. He could not believe his good fortune. After this we got into the boat with the home-made fishing lines and he had the pleasure of catching a few fish. We went back to the billet and talked long into the evening until eventually we had to say goodnight but decided to row him across the lake to the hotel in the moonlight. This was some experience and it must have been very strange to hear English voices singing the boat song that echoed round the valley as we rowed him across and wished him Bon Voyage. He thanked us for having given him such a smashing break from his normal routine and said that we had probably done more for his morale than he had done for ours, and that Billy Butlin would be proud of our camp. Another very happy ship had passed.

It was not long after this that the chap who lived at the other end of the lake, came up to request a prisoner to accompany him the next day as he was going to buy a cow. He had saved up enough money to be able to afford one and was quite look-ing forward to being able to provide enough milk and butter for his family. For reasons unknown to me, he especially requested that I should accompany him, so it was arranged that at six o'clock the next morning I should be at his place ready to go. And so off we went, walking for some miles into an area where there were quite a number of small dairy units where he started asking at the farms if anyone had a cow they could sell. This went on until lunch time when he decided that we could adjourn to one of the watering holes that are spread around in Austria and that people out walking, stop at for liq-uid refreshment and something to eat. There were a number of the local farmers in there who started up a conversation with him and he seemed proud to say this is an English prisoner of war, warning them to be careful what they said as he thought I could understand most of what they were saying. We had a beer and the bread and cheese that he had brought along for lunch before continuing on our quest for another few hours, until he eventually came to a farm that had just what he want-ed. The deal was struck, there and then we put a halter on the very pregnant cow that he had bought, and started the very slow long walk back to his house. It took us about five hours to get back and we arrived at just after midnight. That was a very different experience for me but I do not think that it made us any more friendly. He was still not a man to be trusted, and we were beginning to hear more about the camps that the people disappeared into if they were reported as not supporting the party.

The summer was giving way to autumn and the changes made by the autumn tints, that the leaves took on a this time, meant that the view from the valley was constantly changing to the most beautiful unbelievable sight, that even under our conditions, we could only stand still and admire with the background of dark green conifers, intermingled with the golden, sometimes almost red and brown, from the other trees.

It was around this time, that one afternoon, we were astonished by a very different view. There were two females at the other end of the valley who were not dressed in the manner of all the other local girls, so that we quickly went to find out who they were. We were very surprised to be greeted in very good English and told that they were out looking for wild strawberries. We quickly got into conversation with them to find that they had recently returned to Austria, and had been interned in the Isle of Man from the beginning of the war when they had been working in England. So having heard that there were English prisoners of war in the locality, they had decided that an expedition looking for wild strawberries could be a good excuse to wander up to where we were working.

We soon invited them up to the billet for a cup of tea and for a long chat, that went on and on to dusk. The guards did not seem to mind at all and the girls were quite surprised that we were able to entertain them with a few goodies and some real English tea. As it was getting dusk we told the guards that it would not be correct for them to go back down through the woods alone, and would they permit a couple of us to escort them back to the home of the one who lived in a small village about a couple of miles from St . Wolfgang? They were a little hesitant at the start, but eventually they agreed to this and said that Dicky and I could accompany them, warning us to be very careful how we approached the house at the other end of the lake, and to get back as soon as possible. We quickly split into two pairs — Dicky with the brunette and me with the blonde. We were chatting all the way down the track and onto another track that we had not seen before, till we came out into the fields above the village. There was a bench on which we sat and continued to chat for a while. During the walk down the track I had found out that my companion lived about 40 miles away in Salzburg and was only staying with her friend for a short time. As there would be no future benefit in it, I decided to swop over and was quickly into deep conversation with the brunette who lived in the house nearest to the wood, right on the edge of the village. I arranged to try to get down in the evening a few days later and she agreed that this would be great, and then we wished them both goodnight, and made our way back to the camp. I made a careful mental note of where the track to the village branched off so that I would not get lost in the future.

The summer had been pretty good for us all, and we had all got very fit. We were now getting used to the work that became much easier with experience. The news that we were hearing occasionally was very favourable, even though things were not proceeding as fast as we had hoped after the invasion of the continent. As the autumn progressed we began to realise that we should probably be spending a further winter up in the mountains, and should be getting prepared for this. Johann suggested that we ought to make a few pairs of skis ready for when the snow came. So we went out and selected a suitable ash tree to fell so that it could be used for this purpose, and it was cut into two and a half metre lengths and left for a while to dry out. We provided the money to purchase the fittings that had to be bought and attached to the skis to fasten them to the boots, and then with the help of his expert instructions we were able to make three good pairs of skis. We then were anxiously awaiting the appearance of the snow so that we could practise using them.

I personally was looking forward to the evening's getting dark a little earlier so that it would make it much easier to travel down to the village without being seen. Especially as I would have to pass close to the small house at the other end of the lake if I went to visit my newly-found friend, as I had promised.

I made my first tentative trip that we had arranged, and she was waiting there when I arrived and seemed so glad to have the opportunity to organise how we could communicate and arrange future meetings. She suggested that I should be far less conspicuous if I were to have the Austrian hat and cape that belonged to her brother who was away serving in the forces, and so we returned to her house to collect them.

It is a custom in the mountain villages in Austria that the eligible daughter's bedroom windows are not barred like the rest of the windows in the house, so that they can do their courting in the manner that had been done for very many years, and is known as window tapping. We were able to enter very quietly and spend an enjoyable couple of hours before I made my way back up the mountains and was able to re-enter through the cellar window, from which we had removed the bars. This was the first of many visits that I successfully made down the mountains to the village, but we were having to be extra careful that no-one found out about our friendship. We decided to look for another place where we could meet, especially as her father who was very strict was home at the weekend, even though he worked away during the rest of the week.

There was a watermill on the edge of the stream that ran down the valley close to her house, that did not appear to be used these days of rationing, so we explored the possibility of using this for meetings, and eventually found a way in. It had a very small room with a stove that would have been used by the miller, so we decided that we could make use of this the next time that we met. It was amazing to me to find when I got there, that the place had been thoroughly cleaned and made quite comfortable, and there was also a small stack of firewood at the side of the stove. The miller had a novel way of getting his electric light into the place. We found two wires with hooks on one end by a window and the light bulb at the other end, so when we removed the bulb and hooked the wires onto the mains that passed outside the window, being careful to close the shutters tightly before putting back in the bulb, we then had free electric light.

This was now an ideal meeting place and we would meet there as often as it was possible, on some occasions she would begin with a very nice meal that she had cooked and I was able to enjoy such things as Vienna Schnitzel and Aptfel Strudle, but the winter was approaching fast and there was already a covering of snow on the tops of the highest mountains.

The meeting in the mill had been such a wonderful idea as we were able to relax completely whenever we were inside with all the shutters tightly closed. It came as quite a shock on one occasion in the middle of the night, to hear a horse and cart arrive outside the mill, and then to hear the sluice gate opened to allow the water from the stream to flow through the ducts and on to the waterwheel to set the mill in motion. For a short time there was quite a panic going on to get ourselves presentable and to escape from the building without being seen, but this we were able to do just in time, going out by the window just as the miller was opening the door to bring in the sacks of corn that he was about to grind into flour. He must have had something of a shock also to find hot embers in the fireplace and a comfortable little love nest in what he expected to be a scruffy little room.

I tried looking for some kind of recognition whenever I met one of the farmers later on, to see if they had realised who it was in the mill that night, as the information could have been useful, but at no time did any of them give any indication that they were the illegal miller.

My friends father had not yet prepared his winter supply of firewood and she had the bright idea of telling him that if he applied to the estate agent for the help from a prisoner of war to fell the two trees that he had been allocated and get them ready for taking down to the house, this could be of great help to him (and to us). When the request came I was to be certain that the job was allocated to me, and sure enough this is exactly what happened. I found myself for the following two weekends working with her father, preparing his winter's supply of fuel. On the first Saturday when we were working, she and her sister arrived leading a donkey laden down with a very nice picnic lunch and it became a very pleasant day's work. We had talked it over and decided that it could be a good way of being able to get to visit them on Christmas Day, so that when the father asked what he could give me for helping him I was to say that my wish was to spend a little time with them and a meal at Christmas. He did query if this would be allowed, I assured him that if I was allowed to help him with his work, it would not be a problem to make a visit. This was, of course not at all true, but it worked.

It was around this time that the sentries were changed once again and we unfortunately got a non-smoking ex-customs officer who was not so relaxed as our previous ones had been and always locked up very carefully before counting that we were all safely inside. This made life difficult, but the cellar window became the best way in and out. He did however change the lock on the back door to a lock to which we had a key, that he was not aware of, so that when I returned in the early hours of the morning, I was able to use it and let myself in, then change into my pyjamas and go out through his room saying that I must go to the toilet. I would quickly run round and relock the door before returning through his room. On one occasion it did provide a rather bizarre situation. I was a little careless in passing his window to get to the rear door, and as I came round the side he was standing in the doorway saying "There is someone else out there. I saw them run away as you went out". For the next hour, in the freezing cold, the two of us were looking for an intruder that I knew to be me. When no-one was found, it was quite good for him to apologise to me for having to help him in the cold, and I accepted his apologies very graciously.

The winter was now beginning to close in and the snow line had reached us which created further problems, especially on one evening that I had been visiting and during the time that I had been away we had a pretty good fall of snow that had stopped again by the time that I returned. As I approached the small house at the end of the lake I realised that my footprints in the snow would be a dead giveaway as soon as they were seen, as it would be obvious that someone from the camp had been out. This could bring a lot of complications and needed careful thought, but the solution came to me when I was still some distance away. I turned around and walked backwards until I was some way past the small house, and hoped that when they came out they would think that one of us had had to go to the village early that morning. Then I anxiously awaited any reaction from this the next time I saw our nearest neighbour. There was no reaction and I heaved a great sigh of relief, not just for myself, but also that I had not created a problem for my friends.

The snow was now getting deep enough for the removal of the stacks of timber that we had made, down to the timber yards, and the local farmers arrived one moming with their oxen and heavy sleighs to start the work that they undertook in the winter. We accompanied them up the mountains, each of us with a large long handled shovel to uncover the stacks of timber and help them to load up and get them down into the valley, before setting off in convoy around the lake and down to the village of Strobl. It was quite heavy work but we were able to keep warm with all the exercise. The logs were loaded with one end on the sleigh and the back end dragging on the ground to help to slow the load down on the steep sides of the mountains, but even with chains around the runners it presented great difficulty for the oxen to hold back the load, so that the first part of the journey down was a pretty hairy experience. The farmers had done this many times before and were quite used to the job so that it was about midday when the last one went down track with one very large round tree trunk dragging in the snow and making a miniature cresta run to the bottom of the mountain quite close to the billets. We were all ready to follow them down when Johann said "be patient and we will catch them up in no time at all". So we spent the next half hour cleaning off the snow ready for the next day until he said "Right, now we can go" and sitting down on his shovel with the handle between his legs which he had wrapped around it, he shot off with a yodelling cry and quickly disappeared from view. Brilliant! We thought, this is a new way to travel. We never thought we would be riding on a shovel but it was certainly a surprise, for as soon as we reached the first bend, off we shot into the snow and it took quite a bit of practice before we were able to negotiate the bends without any problem. I had realised that in this part of the world they made the best use of snow for getting around, they even fetched down some of the hay that they had made in the summer on sleighs during the winter. But to ride on a shovel — that certainly was a new experience. The work of moving the timber only lasted a few weeks and we were rapidly approaching Christmas. The weather too was getting progressively worse and most of our time was spent in keeping the track open so that we could get down to the village, but as there was no other work that could be done we were quite happy to set off each morning with our shovels, very similar to the seven dwarfs with a 'hey ho and off to work we go'.

Conditions were getting much worse due to the war situation and food rations were being reduced. It was also decided that we should have a reserve of food in case of emergencies, and a large paper sack full of the old dreaded dried swedes was brought up to us. We really did hope that it would never get so bad that we would resort to eating them again.

I had arranged with my friend that I would go to the Church in St. Wolfgang for the service of the midnight mass that was to be held in the afternoon of Christmas Eve. There was no blackout protection in the church, and afterwards I could make the visit to her home that had been arranged with her father. This did present something of a problem getting down in the daylight, but with the help of the other lads I was able to get away. So, dressed in my Austrian hat and cape, I gingerly approached this very beautiful church in the centre of the town. As I was a little uncertain of the Catholic way, I waited until a lady went into the church and followed her inside, doing all the things exactly as she did, and taking a seat in a pew half way down the church which was slowly filling up with the local people. The few of them that recognised me, did a crafty nod and a wink and were rather amused to see me sitting there. I was amazed at the beauty of the inside of this church, which was unique, in the fact that it had two altars. One had been made to replace the original, but it had been decided that the existing one was much too good to be replaced and the new one was placed in the middle of the church. I could only sit there and try to take in all the wood carvings and ornaments which were so much more beautiful than any I had ever seen before.

When the service started the church was quite full, and in the pew beside me were two German soldiers, one German sailor and one civilian. They did not seem to be aware or interested in the prisoner of war on the end. I did not cause much to be suspicious about as the Christmas hymns that they sang were the ones that I had already learned, especially Stille Nacht, Heillige Nacht, which is known all over the world and originated quite near to where we were. I was able to join in the singing without any fear at all. It was just getting dusk when the service finished and everyone was leaving the church and standing around in little groups in the square around the building. The moon was rising, the air was clear, the lake was frozen over and covered with snow. All around it were the hills and forests that seemed to have an icing on top of them, when the sound from the steeple of the church was of four trumpets playing in harmony the music of Stille Nacht. I cannot describe in words the beauty of this scene, everything was so still, so clear, so cold, so quiet, as if the world had stopped just for us to enjoy this afternoon. The music seemed to leave the building and go completely around this most beautiful Christmas scene. This was such a moving experience to me that will remain so very clear for the rest of my existence. When the music stopped the groups slowly drifted away and I set off along the road towards the house of my friend who with her sister was walking some short distance in front until we got away from the town and were the only ones left, so that we were able to travel together to their home.

We were met at the door by her parents and I was made very welcome. A very nice meal had been prepared that was quite different to what we had for Christmas in England, but nevertheless was very enjoyable, and then we sat around the fire and talked for a couple of hours before I said that I must now return. I wished her father and mother goodbye on doorstep and they watched me go up the track. When I looked back and saw the door had been closed, I turned around and went back and in through the window to the bedroom. It was a little time before my friend was able to say goodnight to her parents and retire to bed, together with her sister who slept in the same room. She was either very tired or a very good actor as very quickly appeared to be sound asleep and we were able to get together and celebrate Christmas in our own special way. The time quickly sped away when I had to return in the very early hours of Christmas day back to the camp.

I have spent Christmas in many different ways during my life, but this was one to remember for such a vastly different variety of reasons.

Winter set in very severely shortly after Christmas and we were totally cut off from the rest of the world. No matter how we tried, it was impossible to clear a track even down to the lake, so that the only thing we could do was to keep warm and hope that the weather would soon break. It turned out to be one of the worst winters that they had had for many years. The stream froze over so that we no longer had running water at the privvy or in the trough and had to use melted snow for everything. We quickly learned to avoid the yellow snow. It snowed every day for the first seven weeks of the year before eventually the sun did manage to come out and begin the process of thawing out. We had long since run out of food and had to resort to the dried swedes which we had twice a day once with garlic and once without, so that it would seem like a change. We were all relieved when we were eventually able to get down to the town, even though it meant a walk of about twice as far as usual as we had to go around the top of the lake and almost into Strobl and along a main road from there to St. Wolfgang. We were now already into March and were pleased to be able to learn of what had been happening in the rest of the world, especially as the progress of our troops in the war had speeded up so much that the end of the war was looking much more imminent.

The last few days of captivity

Chapter 15

FREE AT LAST

In quite a short time we were able to get the track open completely and to go down into town to find out that things had got much worse for the locals, but that the end of the war could not be too far away now as the Russians were advancing fast into Germany and the Yanks and the British had almost completely taken Italy and were advancing towards Austria. Everyone was very anxious that it should not be the Russians that took over their country.

We found that there were quite a number of Red Cross food parcels waiting for us at the post office and were told that this would probably be the last issue that we would get as the question of transport was now quite chaotic. As there were such a large number of them, one of the farmers agreed to transport them up to us on an ox and sleigh. This was an example of the change that was taking place, in the way that we were treated by the local people. They had never treated us badly but now they were able to smile and speak to us when we were in the town in a way that they would never have done previously.

I was able to renew my friendships and need not be quite so careful as I had previously been. Very little work was now being done except for refurbishing the supplies of fuel, and our biggest concern was to try to get the correct news on the position of the troops advancing into Austria. There appeared to be fairly little resistance taking place and it was only occasionally that we heard spasmodic gunfire some long distance away as little pockets of resistance were destroyed.

It became very obvious that at any time now allied troops would reach us, so I decided one morning that I would take some of the food that would have been left, down to my friends to help them. Having delivered it and walked to her place of work, I decided to see what was happening along the main road between St. Wolfgang and Strobl where I met an American patrol of armoured cars led by an officer in a jeep. They pulled up at my side and said "Who the hell are you?" So I informed him that I was a British prisoner of war whose camp was up in the mountains, and that I was out looking for the troops that would release us. Whereupon he said "Do you speak the lingo?" "A little," I answered. "Then climb aboard, we've got to go and get this goddam King". Then reaching for a bottle from underneath his seat, he said "Have a drink of rum!" which of course I did not refuse. Waving the convoy forward, we were soon travelling towards Strobl and during the journey he explained to me that King Leopold of the Belgians was being held in the town, and that their duty was to take prisoner all the guards and release him. We were soon at the large White House in a small town that was completely festooned with white sheets hanging from the highest windows of almost every building. People were lined along the road taking pictures and clapping the arrival of the American troops. I felt quite important sitting up front in the leading vehicle that would mean the war was over for this small country town.

It was quite an experience issuing the orders to the German troops as I was instructed by the American officer and getting them all disarmed and locked into their rooms until they could be transported away. The King and his group came out onto the lawn at the rear of the building and indicated that they were quite happy to stay there until arrangements could be made for them to travel. Then, having got this part all organised and completed we moved on to the local police station where it was my job to explain to the police that they would have to surrender their arms but then to go out on to the streets and keep order.

During the whole of the time there had been the occasional drink of rum from the officer, so that I was now beginning to confuse my languages. It became probably as difficult to understand the American as it was to explain to the Germans. Quite a number of the local troops were taken prisoner during the exercise and some of the German officers were tearing off their badges of rank and identification and were requesting me to explain to the Americans that they were really not bad fellows and should be allowed to go home. But as I had no knowledge of them, they were all taken prisoner to be sorted out later on.

Feeling a little worse for wear I decided that my best course of action was to retire quietly from the scene in the complete confusion and make my way back up to the camp with all this information that I had, so that we could prepare to leave the next day. All the lads were very pleased with the news that I brought them and were pretty busy getting everything together that they would take with them on the journey home. It was agreed that Johann could keep everything that was in the camp that we did not need. One guard had already left to make his own way home which was not too far away, but the senior one had to get back to Munich which meant that he would have to travel through the American lines and would be probably taken prisoner. As he had not been too bad and had with him a civilian suit, we decided that he could accompany us that far as we would need to get transport ourselves.

We decided that we would take the local bus and its driver as far as it was possible, so we made our way into the town saying goodbye to everyone we knew on the way, then boarded the bus and ordered him to take us to Salzburg and drop us off on the motorway out of the town towards Munich. There was only military traffic on the road so we hitched a lift on an American truck that was going to Munich and the driver knew where there was a camp that was an assembling point for all the prisoners of war that were being released.

With great speed we were there, and there were hundreds of other prisoners of war being brought in all the time, all amazed at the wonderful rations that the Americans had enjoyed and finding that they had been accustomed to such little food for such a long time that it was impossible to eat everything that was set before them. It was great to be able to get all the little luxuries that we had missed for so long and to bath, shave, and get really cleaned up to something more respectable. As quickly as it was possible, the prisoners of war were all being flown back to England in the planes that brought in the supplies, or in any space that was available on bombers that were returning to England. We were loaded into huge trucks to transport us down to the airfield driven by big black fellows wearing snow white gloves who thought they were on a race track rather than driving an articulated lorry full of men, but it was a thrill and we enjoyed it .We were then loaded on to a Dacota that ferried supplies from Rheims but as we returned there they were unable to land as the runway had been damaged by a bomb and we had to fly on to Brussels, where we were able to spend the night in an American camp with all the luxuries that they enjoyed including being entertained by a smashing dance band that was stationed there. All the tunes that we used to dance to. Great! Later that day we were told that a fleet of bombers would be landing to refuel before going to England and that we could travel with them, a few in each plane. The pilot decided that as we were coming back we should see the white cliffs of Dover as a welcome home, but as he banked and the white cliffs seem to shoot up the side of plane we were feeling a little air sick and were glad when he flew into Oxfordshire where we landed. We set foot once again on English soil to be welcomed home. There was a large sign over a hangar door saying "WELCOME HOME" and we were led along to this building which was set out with tables and chairs, where we were given a cup of tea, a rock cake, and five fags, and then were liberally sprinkled with louse powder. Quite a welcome home!

Chapter 16
THE DEMOB

The arrival at the reception camp for prisoners of war was certainly a great surprise, at the very efficient manner that the duties were being carried out. Everyone was interviewed and all particulars and information needed was gathered so that the wheels could be set in motion at the same time as we were being cleaned up and issued with a complete new set of kit, which was once again one to wear and one to wash of everything that needed to be washed, together with everything else except firearms.

We were each allocated a bed space for the night and told that we should be away home on leave within 48 hours of our arrival. It was very hard to believe that this could be done, but sure enough after a good night's sleep we were given a new paybook, three months pay, a leave pass for three months, ration cards to cover the period of leave, and a railway ticket to the nearest station to home. We were also able to send a telegram to say the time that we should be arriving.

How times had changed while we had been away, it was all so amazing that within two days of arriving back in England I was once again walking down the street to see a welcome home sign on the front of the house. The next three months were one continuous welcome-home party, meeting the people that I knew, all the family and friends, and attending various functions that had been organised for us. It was a bit embarrassing really, everyone showed so much concern about my welfare. But then expressing some surprise at how well I looked. In what seemed no time at all, the three months had gone and I received instructions to report back to duty with the battalion that was stationed just outside Barnsley, near to a village called Cudworth in Yorkshire.

It was one hell of a shock to be back in the real army again, but as the war in the Far East was still going on we were to be treated rather like new recruits. Our capabilities were to be assessed and then we were to be trained in the modern methods of warfare, which came as quite a shock especially as we had been anticipating our return to civilian life.

The intelligence tests we got really did start at one plus one is two, and C A T spells cat, and they progressed from there. We also had stringent medical tests, as the training that was to come required complete fitness. It was tough! But even though I said I kept getting cold sweats but did not say that it was when I saw the assault courses that awaited us in training, they did not attach any problems with my health to what I had said. It now appeared that life was going to be very rough for the first few weeks, especially when we were told by the previous intake who had been through it, just how difficult and hard everything had become.

A few days after doing my intelligence tests I was told to report to the Quarter Master's office and was wondering what the hell I had done wrong. I smartened myself up and reported to him, when he informed me that he was looking for an office clerk to take charge of the pay sheets, the cigarette and sweet ration issues and to administer these duties. Was I relieved? I could have jumped with joy, but very restrained said that I could probably manage all the duties that were involved. Once again the luck was in — no hard training, no assault courses. I moved my belongings into my own office and found that everybody in the company was making great efforts to be friendly. It was a great position to have and even the staff in the cookhouse turned out to be very obliging, with

127

hot sweet sergeant majors tea in bed in the mornings and very often steak and chips for supper if I stayed in during the evening's. I could not think of a better job in which to serve my time until my demob.

V. J day came and the whole country went crazy, the booze flowed in Barnsley. Barrels of it were really rolled out and a wonderful exciting time was had in celebration.

Demob dates were being started and I learned that it would be at least the middle of 1946 before I would be released, so I bought a motor cycle from a local fellow in order that I could get home for the weekends. Then one day it landed on my desk — my way out. Class B release for tradesmen.

I quickly got the forms and filled them in, to be signed by an officer, and at the same time I filled in a glowing reference for myself, also to be signed. Then I presented them together with many other forms for signature.to the Q M. and with little more than a glance they were signed and quickly despatched.

In little more than a couple of weeks I received orders to join the truck load of fellows to go to York to collect my demob suit, the civilian ration cards, my discharge papers and everything that l needed to return to civvy street the next day. It was hard to believe that I was out!

When my instructions came to report at 8am on Monday morning to a building site in Wolverhampton with my tools to start work on a large council house building project, I quickly realised that it was really true. .

Have there been all those ships in the night? Was it all a dream? Or have I just been demoted from assistant foreman and back on the trowel?